Beach Moose & Amber

# Beach Moose & Amber

## Finding My Jewish History

Sharon Easton

*Beach Moose & Amber*
First edition, April 2023

Beach Moose & Amber Publishing
Nanaimo, British Columbia
sharoneaston.com

Editing: Rachel Dunstan Muller, racheldunstanmuller.com
Self-Publishing Consultant: Cindy Folk, cindyfolkauthor.com
Cover Design: Sarah Lahay, reedsy.com/sarah-beaudin
Interior Formatting: Sarah Lahay, reedsy.com/sarah-beaudin



This is a work of creative nonfiction based on Vera (Nafthal) Goldston's writings, historical research and family and friends' perspective memories. Over time the human memory recall is not always precise. Family information was limited; therefore, some events were pieced together with historical research and may not be entirely factual. The dialogue between relatives is purely fictional with the exception of the author's personal involvement. This story is as true to the facts as possible. The author and publisher take no responsibility for any discrepancies in the information found in this book.

ISBN: 978-1-7779421-0-6

*Before the Holocaust my mother holidayed at her grandfather's cottage in the village of Schwartzort on the Curonian Spit, where the elite — both Jews and Gentiles from Germany and Lithuania went to play. There were wild moose roaming on the beaches and a moose sanctuary on the peninsula. The beaches were also famous for their amber and my mother had a large amber collection which she had to leave behind when they fled.*

*My mother's childhood and my childhood collided — moose have always been my favorite wild animal and the orange/yellow amber occurring from the Baltic Sea is a common color of my birthstone —Topaz. Mom never talked about her past, so I never knew these stories.*

All I ask you is not to forget me.

-VERA OLGA (NAFTHAL) GOLDSTON, 1990

*Dedicated to my daughters, Heather and Sarah,*
*and my grandson, Joshua, and for any others born after you.*
*This family history is my gift to you. I have done everything in my*
*power to track our family's many secrets to bring you this story,*
*but the whole truth is gone with your ancestors.*
*As you move through life, may you know that your family tree is*
*filled with strong people and that their strength is your inheritance.*
*With all my heart and unconditional love always.*

# Contents

# Nafthal / Isserlin Family Tree

*Note: As not to confuse the reader, the family trees only represent the Nafthal/Isserlin immediate family members — and the tree ends in the mid-1930s. There, were, and are, so many more family members.*

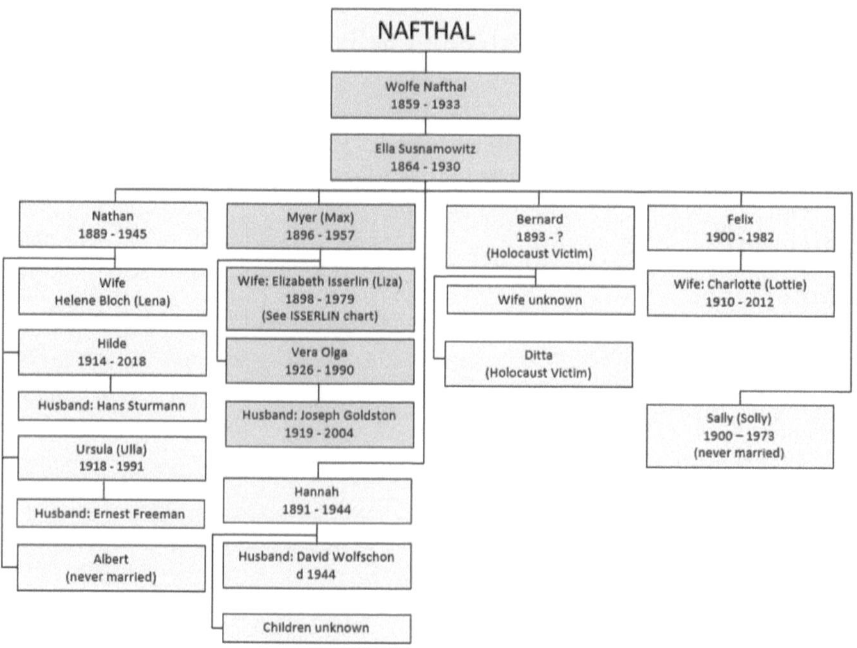

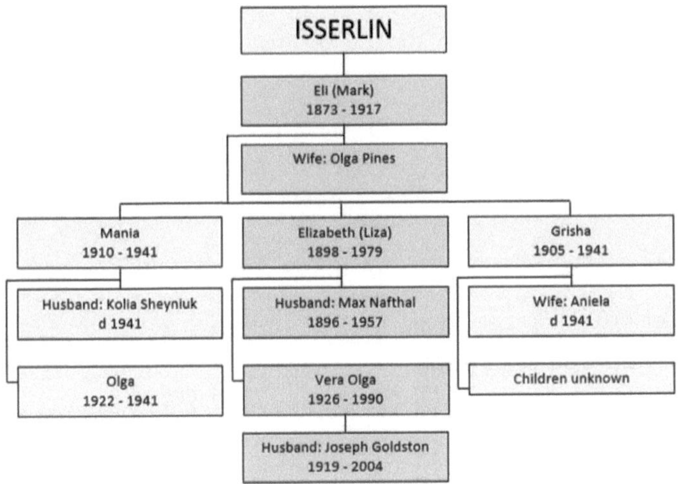
ISSERLIN
Eli (Mark)
1873 - 1917
Wife: Olga Pines
Mania
1910 - 1941
Elizabeth (Liza)
1898 - 1979
Grisha
1905 - 1941
Husband: Kolia Sheyniuk
d 1941
Husband: Max Nafthal
1896 - 1957
Wife: Aniela
d 1941
Olga
1922 - 1941
Vera Olga
1926 - 1990
Children unknown
Husband: Joseph Goldston
1919 - 2004

# Map of Europe 1929-1939[1]

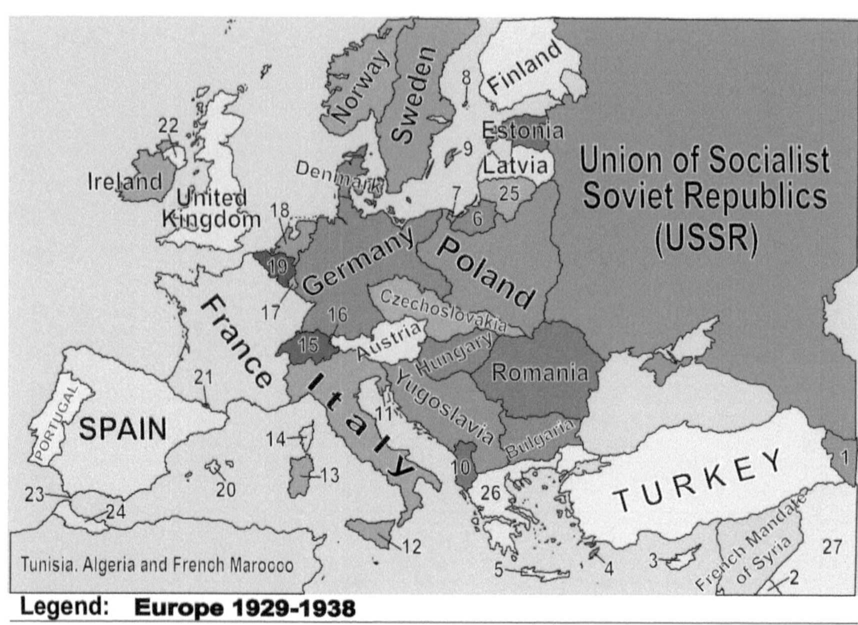


**Legend: Europe 1929-1938**

1) Persia (Iran)
2) British Mandate of Palestine
3) Cyprus (British Crown Colony)
4) Rhodes and Dodecanese (Italy)
5) Crete (Greece)
6) East Prussia (Germany)
7) Free City of Danzig
8) Aland Islands (Finland)
9) Gotland (Sweden)
10) Albania
11) Istria (Italy)
12) Sicily (Italy)
13) Sardinia (Italy)
14) Corsica (France)
15) Switzerland
16) Liechtenstein
17) Luxembourg
18) Netherlands
19) Belgium
20) Balearic Islands (Spain)
21) Andorra
22) Northern Ireland (UK)
23) Gibraltar (British Crown Colony)
24) Spanish Marocco (Spain)
25) Lithuania
26) Greece
27) British Mandate of Iraq

Source: https://commons.wikimedia.org/wiki/File:EUROPE_1929-1938_POLITICAL_MAP.svg

# Map of Lithuania 1939[2]

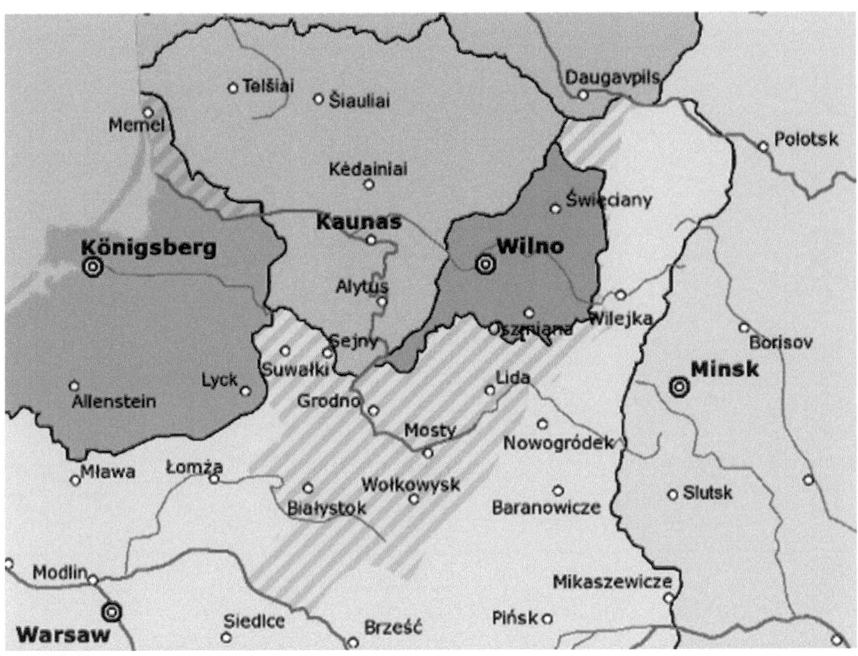


Source: https://commons.sikimedia.org/wiki

# Map of Nova Scotia, Present Day

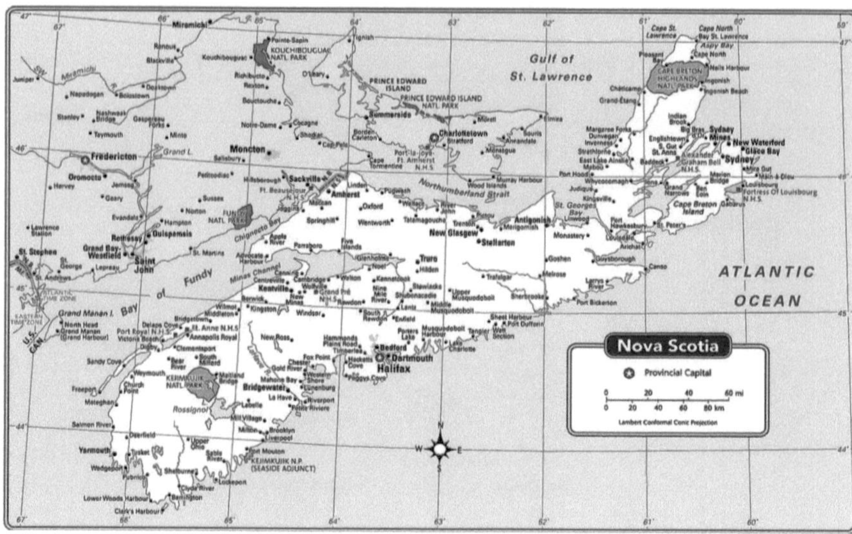


Source: https://www.worldatlas.com/maps/canada/nova-scotia [3]

# Prologue

I don't remember anyone telling me I was Jewish; I just knew. That said, I had no idea what being a Jew even meant — no one told me. Both sides of our family tree were Jewish as far back as I could go. But I never knew those relatives.

It never occurred to me to write a story about my family history. I always knew the past held terrifying secrets. Most times my family didn't talk about their earlier lives. For no apparent reason and at the oddest moments, however, my mother or grandmother would occasionally offer me a glimpse into the past, leaving me to wonder.

In 2004, my father passed away thirteen years after my mother's death. My siblings and I were left with the daunting task of closing down my parents' home. We created a small 'toss pile' in Dad's den. Among the rejected items, I picked up a worn accordion file folder. The stretchy band around the file remained intact, although much of its elasticity was gone. The folder reminded me of Dad, who often carried it in the crook of his arm. When I walked away from Dad's house that day, I had no idea I was carrying away small pieces of what would become my greatest writing adventure.

Over the next thirteen years, I often used Dad's folder to protect my writing from bent corners and raindrops. The old folder managed to make its way into a packing box each time I moved.

During our last move in 2015, I came across my father's old folder and discovered a forgotten collection of my short stories and notes. I opened the accordion file even wider, and to my surprise, I found unfamiliar papers in the back. I soon realized I was holding pieces of my mother's memories and experiences, written shortly before her death.

I wasn't surprised to discover disjointed bits of information that seemed to be nothing much at all. Frustrated with more family secrets, I put the notes back into their hiding place and stored the file in a cupboard — promptly forgetting it.

A year later, I picked up my dad's tattered folder and reread my mother's papers. Surprisingly, this time Mom's jumbled notes made sense. She had typed these words.

> For many years I have wanted to write a book on our family history. Probably the main reason I did not do so was that I did not have the talent or the know-how. So now it is a bit late. I'll put down as many of the old family stories as I can, and maybe your dad will in time do the same with his family and war stories. And maybe some day in years to come one of your children or grandchildren may develop a talent as a writer and thus incorporate some of this material in a book. If not, maybe when our grandchildren are a bit older, they will enjoy reading about their family history.
>
> All I ask from you is not to forget me.
>
> —VERA OLGA (NAFTHAL) GOLDSTON

This was the complete opposite of what Mom had led me to understand. Mom had always believed that a life passed should be forgotten; it was better to move on. I could not trust her written words. I read them over and over again. Despite what she'd told me, I finally knew for sure that Mom had never forgotten a single person after their death. Most of the deaths my mother had experienced were horrific murders, and she had so many to remember.

Written at a time so close to Mom's passing, I began to appreciate her effort to break down her lifelong wall of silence, to tell her story in the hope — she would not be forgotten. With my mother's written consent, I knew the moment had come. It was time to break the silence, to share the family's secrets. Within minutes of reading Mom's papers, and without realizing what I was taking on, there was no turning back.

Mom's words were right — it was too late for her to tell the whole story. There wasn't much information in the pages she had written, or so I thought at first. But once I'd organized her writing, I realized Mom had left enough material to start a little research. I did the only thing I felt I could in this matter — I began exploring my family's past. I picked everything apart and slowly began to piece the story back together — matching Mom's bits of information to historical events. My story is based on my maternal side of the family.

I never talked about my mother or grandparents to anyone except my daughters and grandson. And even that was not often. I sat in silence for long periods, my mind full of memories of my mother, grandmother and grandfather. I started with my grandmother's horrifying involvement in Russia during World War I (WWI) and the Russian Revolution, and then I quickly moved on to her new life in Lithuania, leading up to World War II (WWII) and the Holocaust. Once I started, I couldn't stop.

At first, I thought I would do a little research and write a few short stories. That's all. I would share them with my writing group, or might even burn them — forever gone. I started by sharing a few funny stories about my mother. People loved her and always wanted more. Next, I took a deep breath, and the real work began. I had to learn how to talk about my family's silence. As I dove deeper into the family's past, I realized this wasn't just my mother's story; it was the collective story of my grandparents, aunts, uncles and cousins as well.

And so began a remarkable journey.

---

I have included pieces of my mother Vera Olga (Nafthal) Goldston's final written pages at the beginning of some chapters.

Under the line, at the end of some chapters — I have recorded my thoughts, memories, and my emotional feelings generated by writing this book. Recognizing that my four siblings' thoughts and memories are theirs to share — or not — these notes primarily represent my personal understanding. Everyone remembers events differently; everyone has their version of a story. With the facts that I gathered from my mother's written pages, supplemented by research, information collected from historians, and the contributions of family and friends, this is my interpretation of my family's journey.

## Chapter 1

# Liza

> Where to start, that is hard to know. Let me tell you a bit about my mother's background.
>
> —VERA OLGA (NAFTHAL) GOLDSTON

**ELIZABETH ISSERLIN WAS BORN** during one of Russia's most horrific periods, but then who among us can choose the date of our birth? Being born Jewish made matters even more challenging, though the Isserlin family was not particularly religious. People envied her rich beginnings, believing that because Elizabeth was fortunate enough to be born into an affluent family, her future would be filled with excitement, happiness and wealth. Little did they know.

Olga and Eli Isserlin welcomed Elizabeth into the world on July 20, 1898. Sometime after her birth, she acquired the nickname Liza[4], which stuck throughout her life. Liza was her parents' second child; she had an older sister, Mania, born three years earlier, and a younger brother, Grisha, born five years later.

In the late 19th and early 20th centuries, Russian Jews experienced difficult times as the result of political prejudice. Most Jewish people suffered from poor health, poverty and segregation. Members of the Isserlin family were a rarity among Russian Jews. Thanks to their wealth, upper-class Europe opened its doors and welcomed them in.

Liza seldom talked about her childhood. She believed that the past cannot be changed, and therefore is best forgotten.

---

Our family tree includes great rabbis. Rabbi Jehiel Luria is particularly notable as the first rabbi of Brisk, Poland (late 1400s - 1500s). His grandson Rema Rabbi Moshe Isserles (Feb. 22, 1530 - May 11, 1572) was a prominent Talmudist and independently wealthy. The Talmud is the primary source of Jewish religious law and theory; a Talmudist is a specialist in Talmud studies. Most Jewish communities use the Talmud as a foundation for Jewish daily and cultural life, including aspirations. My ancestor was one of the greatest Jewish scholars of all time, and he left many writings behind when he passed. Rema Rabbi Moshe Isserles was buried in Remah Cemetery, the Old Jewish Cemetery of Krakow, Poland.

During the occupation of Poland in WWII, Nazis destroyed this gravesite. They tore down walls and hauled away tombstones to use as paving stones in concentration camps or to sell for profit. Rabbi Isserles' stone is one of the few that remained intact.[5]

I was surprised to discover such a famous rabbi in our family tree, dating back to the 1400s. Eli and Olga Isserlin and their children were not overly religious, and by the time I was born, my grandmother and mother didn't talk about Jewish beliefs. The exception was my grandmother lighting a Yahrzeit[6] lamp on the anniversary of my grandfather's death — a common Jewish custom to pay tribute to a life passed. The light had a tiny Star of David[7] inside its narrow bulb. Keeping the light burning signifies that the memory of the deceased lives on, still burning bright. As a young child, my grandmother was firm about not turning the lamp off and on. Traditionally, a Yahrzeit light is only lit for twenty-four hours, but my grandfather's light remained burning for seven days. Perhaps my grandmother had too many memories to contain in a single day.

My mother never lit a Yahrzeit lamp for anyone with the exception of her parents. So many loved ones had passed, that if she had lit a lamp for each one, the lighting would have been endless.

Chapter 2

# Eli Isserlin's Fortune

> My grandparents were Eli [Mark] and Olga Isserlin. My grandfather was a wealthy merchant in St. Petersburg.
>
> —VERA OLGA (NAFTHAL) GOLDSTON

**For a Jewish man** and his family, nothing was more important than survival. This required money.

In 1873, Eli Isserlin was born into old, Jewish money in Vilna, Lithuania. Nothing else is known about Eli's life until he relocated to Libau, Russia, where he became a successful merchant selling fine porcelain and Chanel #5 Perfume.

As an adventurous and ambitious man, Eli was interested in St. Petersburg, Russia's capital, which had become a centre for business and entertainment in Russia and Europe. Responding to city officials who provided unlimited opportunities to attract wealthy Russian Jews, Eli relocated his family and business to St. Petersburg, where he became even more successful. His wife, Olga, established herself as a member of high society, spending her days managing her home, children and servants.

Although affluent Jewish people were thriving in the business world, as a religious group Jews were not popular and faced discrimination. As a result, many Jews changed their first and sometimes family names to conceal their heritage. Since a Hebrew name could mean a tragic end to his thriving business, and since failure was never an option for Eli, he quickly changed his name to Mark. Mark Isserlin knew that a wealthy man could grow even wealthier; it was just a matter of being in the right place, at the right time.

Around 1910, Mark travelled from St. Petersburg to Paris by train for business. He shared a compartment with an Englishman, the vice-president of The Gramophone Co. Ltd, later known as His Master's Voice (RCA Victor).[8] During the journey, the two men were drawn to each other, to the extent that they would ultimately become lifelong friends. Mark's new acquaintance presented him with a business proposal, to become the agent for His Master's Voice, either in the United States or for all of Russia. The offer was too good to refuse.

As an adventurous man, Mark wanted to go to America, but pressure from his parents kept him in Russia. No matter how old or independent a person was, in those days you did what your parents wanted. In the early 20$^{th}$ century, no one left Europe for America unless necessary. Mark did not need to leave. He accepted the agency for all of Russia — a decision that would prove fatal in the years to come.

Mark returned to his home in St. Petersburg. But one evening, he did not appear for dinner at the expected time. Much to the cook's distress, the family meal sat waiting in the kitchen. Olga paced back and forth in the parlour as the evening stretched on and Mark remained missing. The cook continued to stand over her pots and platters, watching her dinner go to ruin. Finally, Olga could wait no more. Along with a servant, she sent her daughter, Liza, and young son Grisha, to the family's shop to look for their father.

The children could not get near the store. The streets were crammed with people listening to the first recorded music in Russia which came from a His Master's Voice phonograph — proudly displayed in the front window of their father's shop. Needless to say, Mark became a very wealthy man.

---

Mark Isserlin was my great-grandfather, but I only know him through my research into my family's journey. How do I explain how much I love him when I never knew him. I cannot.

Liza Isserlin, Mark's daughter, was my maternal grandmother — and I adored her.

Nanny never talked about her life before emigrating from Lithuania. For instance, she never told me about our strong family connection to Chanel #5. Even though I was unaware of the family link, this had been my favourite fragrance for many years, until perfume became socially unacceptable. When I read my mother's pages decades later, I was devastated that Nanny had never spoken of our connection to Chanel #5.

I also loved wearing my grandmother's favourite rose-scented body cream along with the perfume, creating my own unique fragrance. After all these years, I wonder if the Chanel I wore triggered painful memories for Nanny. This led to many sleepless nights. My understanding of my family's silence began to take on a new depth.

Chapter 3

# The Unhappiness of the People

> My grandparents were wealthy merchants who were permitted to live outside the Pale of Russia. The Pale consisted of areas where Jews were allowed to live in shetls [little towns]. And unless you were wealthy enough to buy your way out or talented in some way to serve the Russian aristocracy, or very well educated, you were condemned to spend your life in such a shetl. My mother's family, that is her immediate family of parents and grandparents, all lived outside the Pale as far as I know. But of course, most Jews still had distant family there and helped them with cash, to escape conscription into the Czar's army, and to emigrate whenever they could. The rich relatives helped the poor.
>
> -VERA OLGA (NAFTHAL) GOLDSTON

**WWI and the Russian** Revolution are extremely complex events, and a brief understanding of the conditions of these times is critical.

These details will help explain the fate of the Isserlin family and their fortune.

At the beginning of the 20th century, Russia was politically corrupt. The ruler, Tsar Nicholas II, held complete power over the Russian people. He controlled the churches, the army, and the early rail system, all with an iron fist. His wealth and power extended throughout the country. The poor, unpopular Jews received the worst parcels of land.

Throughout the western region of Imperial Russia, impoverished Jews were forced to live within "The Pale of Settlement." The Pale included several designated areas with varying boundaries scattered throughout western Russia. They were isolated wastelands with no means of farming, nor employment. Poorly built shacks were quickly constructed by the Jews from whatever wood, rock and sticks could be found on the land. The hovels provided little protection from the freezing winters or blazing, hot summers.

The Pale was originated as a means of segregating disadvantaged Jews from the remaining Russian population. Mark Isserlin and his family received special permission from the Russian government to live outside the walls of the Pale. This privilege was given sparingly and only to the most affluent, influential Jews.

Wealthy members of the synagogues supported the poor with *tzedakah*, a form of traditional Jewish charity. The *tzedakah* provided clothing, free medical care for the sick and dying, and even dowries and household gifts for young brides. Without this charity, thousands of Jews would have perished. Wealthy Jews also funded schools within The Pale. Only boys were educated — even the brightest girls were forbidden an education. Girls were raised to be good, obedient wives to their future husbands.

Poverty existed all over Russia. Poor Russian Gentiles suffered from similar fates as the Jews. They received low wages and paid high rents in overcrowded slums, often with five to seven residents living in one small room. In both the Pale and the slums of Russia, open sewers created critical sanitation and health issues, often leading to premature death. Poor weather conditions and a lack of suitable clothing brought misery to everyone. Empty stomachs could not provide enough energy for a healthy labourer or a nursing mother. The population of uneducated and impoverished Jews and Gentiles exploded across the country.

The disadvantaged were powerless against the government on their own, and so in time leaders among the underprivileged began to form organizations. Jews and Gentiles agreed they needed to come together. They would seek support for higher wages and improved safety conditions at work to generate healthier circumstances.

Despite the deplorable conditions of this period, the Russian people adored and respected Tsar Nicholas II, their ruler and head of the regime. They blamed all their misfortunes on the government until one fatal day changed everything. The Isserlin family did not realize it at the time, but these events would change their destiny forever.

In 1904, thousands of Russian peasants and working-class labourers signed a document demanding improved working conditions. On Sunday, January 9, 1905, many thousands of people dressed in the black garb of the times fought their way through high snowdrifts to the Moscow Gate. In a peaceful demonstration for the betterment of their lives, they pressed deeper towards the centre of the city on their way to the Tsar's White Palace to make their plea. The people anticipated the Tsar's sympathies. At times, women and children led the march, their spirits running high with hopes of a better future.

They were met instead with unexpected rage. The Tsar did not even make an appearance. With a clenched jaw and tight fists, he commanded the military to fire on the unarmed, peaceful demonstrators. The soldiers turned on their people, which resulted in two hundred needless deaths and eight hundred injuries. The people named this day 'Bloody Sunday,' and now saw the Tsar as the enemy.

The Tsar rapidly lost the affections of his people, and the seeds of a revolution began to grow. Demonstrations began with a small series of strikes while the anger of the people grew and spread throughout Russia. Mark Isserlin was aware that a revolution was coming. During dinner discussions, Mark and his friends kept the family well informed as these events occurred. At the tender age of seven, Liza was already beginning to understand the politics of her country.

Chapter 4

# World War I and the Russian Revolution

> When World War I broke out, my mother and all her family got trapped in Germany. They spent a week in a corner of the Palace in Konigsberg. Finally, they were exchanged for German tourists travelling in Russia.
>
> -VERA OLGA (NAFTHAL) GOLDSTON

**Before the Revolution, Mark's** oldest daughter, Mania, married a man named Kolia Sheyniak. The couple moved to London, England, where Kolia worked for the Thomas Hedley Soap & Candle Company.[9] Mark and Olga's two younger children, Liza and Grisha, still lived at home, which was now in Moscow.

In 1914, Liza was sixteen years old and a real beauty. When WWI broke out, the Isserlin family was travelling in Germany. Given that Russia and Germany were now on opposite sides, the Isserlins were declared prisoners of war and held in Konigsberg Castle.[10] Mark suffered from severe anxiety, fearing for the safety of his family. Within a week, Germany and Russia negotiated an exchange — the Isserlin family for German travellers detained in Russia. The family returned to Moscow unharmed.

The Great War and the Russian Revolution affected all citizens, rich and poor. In the first three years of WWI, two million Russian soldiers were needlessly killed in battle, and another five million were wounded. Even more, people would die during the Revolution.

The Isserlin family, along with other affluent Jews, supplied the soldiers with kosher[11] food, clothes and shoes — but they were powerless against the regime to help in any other way. The country was in an uproar. The Russian people blamed the deaths of their young men on the unpopular Tsar and demanded revenge.

In early 1917, Russia's peasants and labourers came together and revolted against their poor living conditions, resulting in many strikes. Once again, the Tsar commanded the Russian army to quell the uprisings with violence. Unlike 'Bloody Sunday' in, 1914, the army, largely made up of peasants and labourers, refused to fire on their countrymen. This was the beginning of mutiny against the Tsar. The army forced the Tsar to give up his throne, his wealth, and all his lands.

These were difficult times for the Isserlin family.

Much to her mother and father's disapproval, Liza, now nineteen-years-old, would often leave her home to witness events first-hand. The wealthy were unpopular with the poor working class, and the crowds might have harmed or even killed her if they knew her true identity — so Liza would disguise herself as a maid. Olga had lost all control over her daughter as Liza insisted on making her way to the crowded public squares, including Moscow's famous Red Square. There she listened to the great speakers of the time.

In August 1917, Liza was in St. Petersburg. The city was in chaos. Tsar Nicholas II had completely lost public support due to extreme food shortages which had led to starvation. People resented the Tsar for not resolving their hardship and not leading the country efficiently — and so the Russian Communist Party (Bolsheviks)[12] forced the Tsar to abdicate his throne. Liza was in St Petersburg Square the day Tsar Nicholas II, his family, and their entourage were all forcefully taken from the Winter Palace. It was a dangerous place for a wealthy Jewish girl. Liza did not see the royal family but was aware of these events. Life in Russia was becoming more dangerous every day.[13]

Knowing the Revolution threatened his family's lives and wealth, Mark worried constantly and his health began to suffer. Affluent Jews were losing their businesses, homes and money to the Revolution. It was impossible to leave the country, and Mark had no place to hide his family or their fortune. They lived in constant fear.

The Isserlin family could feel their good life slipping away. Nonetheless, Liza chose to face the Revolution straight on.

---

My sister Janet told me the story about Nanny being in St. Petersburg Square when the Tsar and his family were forcefully taken from the Winter Palace. In 1967, Janet and Nanny were visiting Boston and went to see the movie *Dr. Zhivago.* The story takes place during WWI and the Russian Revolution. Janet believed the movie took Nanny back to those horrific days.

On a historical note, the novel *Dr. Zhivago* by Boris Pasternak was awarded the Nobel Prize for Literature in 1958. The Soviet government refused to allow Pasternak to accept the honour and the book was banned throughout Russia. Pasternak was expelled from the Soviet Writer's Union.

Chapter 5

# Survival

> Left alone with Grisha, a few things to sell, all cash etc. confiscated, my mother [Liza] made her way slowly towards a Russian Border. Jewellery which she did not take they hid over the doorjambs and it is possible if the house had not been bombed that those jewels still sit there, in any way no good to anyone. [home unknown] So she and Grisha made their way to a border town where the Reds and Whites battled over a bridge and they bided their time.
>
> -VERA OLGA (NAFTHAL) GOLDSTON

**Mark knew the Revolution** was dangerous for the wealthy and even worse for the affluent and unpopular Jews. The Russian Revolution's philosophy of taking from the rich and giving to the poor was of great concern. This resulted in dangerous conditions and damaging financial consequences for the Isserlin family.

War combined with the Revolution led to a famine. The Isserlin money did very little to help feed the family. Fearless Liza often took her bicycle into the country to purchase eggs at a hugely inflated cost.

The losses began to take a toll on Mark's health. Early in 1917, at age forty-four, Mark died of a heart attach and his brother died soon afterward. Olga was never the same after her husband's death. She contracted Typhus Fever, which ran rampant throughout Russia, and died shortly after. Liza wore the traditional black in mourning for years, but she hated it. Although she followed tradition, she preferred the custom of the white or light-coloured clothing normally worn by the wealthy outside of mourning.

When her parents died, nineteen-year-old Liza became responsible for her sixteen-year-old brother, Grisha. Her twenty-three-year-old sister, Mania, and Mania's husband, Kolia, still lived in London, England. They tried to help, but because Liza and Grisha were behind the Russian border, nothing could be done. The government seized the family business and home, including all furnishings and valuables, and froze the family's bank accounts. Everything was gone. Shocked and penniless Liza and Grisha sat in their ransacked home that the Russian government now owned.

Liza planned to take Grisha and reunite with Mania in England. She was resilient and determined that they would survive. Most importantly, the siblings were young, bright and reasonably healthy.

A last look through their home brought hope. Liza discovered the family jewels had been overlooked when their properties and other valuables were seized. The jewels were worth a fortune, but Liza knew they couldn't be sold for much-needed cash, nor safely carried on their journey. To save the family jewels, Liza hid them in the door jams of their home. After carefully removing the door casings, she and her brother wrapped the jewels in linen and old paper and stuffed the valuables in the gap between the door jambs and the frames. When the casings were replaced, everything looked the same as before — their hidden treasure would be safe. When the Revolution was over, they planned to return and reclaim their wealth.

One morning, Liza and Grisha dressed in rags to disguise themselves. Then each carrying a small satchel, they walked out the front door of the family home for the last time. There was no need to lock up because government officials and demonstrators would break down the door and steal whatever they could find. Without looking back, the siblings walked away. Although they missed their parents, other family members and friends, thoughts of their survival soon consumed them.

Chaos was everywhere. Law and order no longer existed in Russia. As they made their way through the country, Liza and Grisha were far from alone — thousands of women, children and armed men trudged across cities, towns and villages. More than six million displaced persons tried to escape the fighting, including Jews, Gypsies[14], Poles, Ukrainians and Germans. Liza and Grisha made their long journey to the border by any method they could: accepting rides on horse-drawn carts, jumping onto moving trains, but most often walking.[15] Staying out of sight was their most important strategy. This was not always an easy task with so many citizens and soldiers on the move, but they managed. Most of all they hid from Russian soldiers, who killed all Jews who crossed their path. But soldiers were not the only ones to fear during their travels.[16]

At the beginning of the Great War, most Russian citizens had empathy for evacuated refugees. By 1917, however, compassion had disappeared, since refugees had no food and no money for lodging.[17]

Government control vanished. Critical shortages of all the necessities led to soaring inflation on the black market. Thieves and bandits hid everywhere, waiting for innocent victims. They took food, clothing and coal, leaving the refugees with nothing.[18] With law and order non-existent, Liza and Grisha trusted no one.

The siblings endured poor nutrition and contaminated water, and their health began to suffer. With so many displaced people crowding the railways and riverbanks Cholera and Typhus Fever spread rapidly throughout the population.[19] Dead bodies were left where they dropped. Often a dead person's clothing, shoes, and valuables were taken before the body was cold.[20]

Liza and Grisha finally arrived at a border where Red and White armies were battling over a bridge. During WWI, the boundaries changed often. Without any legal documentation and continuous fighting, it was impossible for Liza and Grisha to cross. Instead, they kept hidden while they waited for a safe moment to slip over the border.

The siblings were in trouble. With no money left for food, Liza and Grisha hunted in the garbage. Grisha could eat any trash, from rotten potatoes to moldy bread — even stinking herring. But though her brother begged, Liza could not eat and began to waste away. Grisha was afraid she would starve to death.

Every day the siblings waited for their opportunity. Finally, there was a lull in the fighting on the bridge, and the guards disappeared from the border crossing. Liza and Grisha took a deep breath and slipped across the bridge to freedom. They had finally escaped Russia's iron grip.

Once across the border, Liza and Grisha were helped by committees from private charities and local government agencies offering aid to refugees.[21] Back in England, Mania and Kolia were informed of Liza and Grisha's successful escape. Mania immediately wired money for train tickets, boat fare, lodging and food, and Liza and Grisha quickly made their way to London to reunite with their sister. But both arrived in poor health — especially Liza.

London had endless food, in stark contrast to Russia's famine. Liza was offered an array of tasty treats, but nothing stayed down. As a result of her slow, near-starvation, Liza suffered lung problems for several years. Throughout her life, gut issues would also plague her — a painful reminder of the losses she'd endured.

---

A century later, it's impossible to know where this bridge was located or which country the siblings entered when they walked out of Russia. Sadly, this information is lost.[22]

---

I wonder if Nanny's horrendous memories of the Russian Revolution were not as suppressed as I always thought. I wish I'd asked more questions. Perhaps she would have realized I was interested. Maybe it would have made a difference.

And what happened to the Isserlin fortune? The authorities kept all the wealth for themselves. They stole all businesses, homes and assets from the Isserlin family, and many other wealthy Jews. But since the government officials did not have a good understanding of enterprise, these confiscations ended in financial disaster.

Liza and Grisha never returned to Russia.

Chapter 6

# The Nafthal Family Circa 1910

> My grandfather [on my father's side] was Wolfe Nafthal. He was a very kind gentleman, a very orthodox Jew who never even ate at the home of any of his children because they were not kosher. All our family meals and holidays were held at his house. My grandmother Ella was hospitalized for some time. She came home for a while and had Felix; then back to the hospital; then back home and had Sally. But shortly after she was permanently hospitalized and only came for rare visits. All I remember was that I was scared to death of her. So my Opapa, [grandfather], with the help of a very Orthodox housekeeper, brought up his family. I am sure he had a hard time of it. But all grew up. So your grandfather [Max] was brought up in a large, lively family.
>
> VERA OLGA (NAFTHAL) GOLDSTON

**Wolfe Nafthal was born** into an affluent, Orthodox Jewish family, but nothing is known of his childhood. In 1864, he moved his family to Memel,[23] (Klaipeda), in Memelland Territory,[24] Lithuania. There he was the owner and operator of the Wolfe Nafthal Company, a steam-powered sawmill on the right bank of the Dange River, now the Dane River. The family home in Memel was located at 3 Liepu Street. They also owned two other properties on the same street, numbers 4 and 6 Liepu Street.

Wolfe Nafthal was a well-loved and respected man known for his generosity and fairness. His wife, Ella, was the love of his life — even though the relationship had challenges. Ella suffered from a serious mental illness and spent most of her life in and out of a mental institution.

Wolfe doted on his wife in spite of her illness. He often brought Ella home from the hospital for short periods. These visits resulted in her last two children, their son Felix, and then their last son, Sally (pronounced "Solly" in German). After Sally's birth, Ella was permanently hospitalized with only short and rare visits home.

Wolfe employed a loyal, Orthodox Jewish housekeeper, who helped raise his six sons and one daughter: Nathan, Bernard, Meyer (Max, my grandfather), Leo, Felix, Hanna and Sally. Sadly, Leo committed suicide over a love affair gone bad before WWII.

Meyer was born in June 1896, at the family cottage in the village of Schwartzort[25] on the Curonian Spit. The cottage was the family's gathering place for many years. Schwartzort was located at the southern end of the spit close to East Prussia. The spit was a long, narrow cape that belonged to Lithuania. It was a beautiful resort area, where the elite of Lithuania and Germany owned cottages or visited luxury hotels and resorts on the sunny beaches of the Baltic

Sea. To this day, the Curonian Spit remains a popular vacation area.

Wolfe worried about Meyer's future. As a young lad of fifteen, Meyer was no different than any other boy — he thought he knew everything. But Meyer's failing school marks told his father another story. Although he was bright, the boy knew nothing. Wolfe was aware his son had learning problems — Meyer did not respond to traditional teaching methods. For Wolfe, failure was not an option. He believed that he had no other choice but to take his son out of school. Wolfe had made a fortune in the timber business. He hoped the trade was in his son's blood as well and decided to find out.

Meyer was set up in an apprenticeship with a well-respected timber company. The boy boarded with an Orthodox Jewish household, but the poor family never had enough money to feed him well. He was always hungry, and the situation soon became critical. Meyer could not concentrate on his work and no longer enjoyed his apprenticeship. He soon showed up on his father's doorstep.

Wolfe could not hide his surprise. "What are you doing here?" he asked his son.

"I'm starving to death. I can't think! My stomach is always empty. I can't learn. I need food!" The cook was outraged because Meyer was hungry and thrilled at the same time. She had Meyer back at her dining room table again.

"So many complaints from this boy," thought Wolfe. He watched his son down a plate of sausages, sauerkraut and heavy German rye bread — just to hold him over until dinner. But Wolfe was not ready to give up on his son's future, so he quickly came up with a second plan.

Wolfe sent Meyer back to his apprenticeship — but this time, he boarded his son with a butcher's family, where there was always an abundance of good food. The butcher's wife was an excellent cook and enjoyed feeding Meyer until he was full. He not only began to learn about the timber business, he soon discovered a love for it.

Wolfe made another decision in favour of his son's future. In those days, companies owned by Gentiles did not want to admit they had business dealings with Jews. To keep his son's Jewish heritage hidden, Wolfe renamed Meyer. For business purposes, he would now be called "Max." Meyer loved his new name, and from that day forward, he was known as Max wherever he went.

Max worked hard and proudly proved himself to be the firm's top apprentice — although he nearly got himself tossed out. It all started when the main office developed a terrible stink. The complaints came in from the top foremen down to the inexperienced labourers. The smell grew so strong, that workers refused to go into the office to get their paperwork signed; they only entered when their jobs were threatened. Customers walked out in the middle of discussions, claiming they needed fresh air. The stench created constant chaos within the firm. Max was the only person who did not seem to notice the overpowering smell. Then one day, the mystery was solved.

Max was sitting at his desk. He looked around quickly to ensure no one was there, then slid open his top drawer and lifted some papers to reveal a large wedge of stinky cheese. He broke off a piece and was about to pop it into his mouth when the boss walked up behind his desk. The humid heat of summer — along with an absence of refrigeration, air conditioning, or ventilation in the small, primitive office space resulted in all sorts of unpleasant odours. The dreadful smell of hoarded, stinky cheese was too much to bear. His boss' discovery ended the cheese era for Max. He could have been fired, but given his dedication to the timber business, he received a strong warning instead. Max continued his apprenticeship with great success.

---

The source of my great-grandmother Ella's mental illness was never mentioned; this critical piece of family information is lost forever.

My grandfather, Max, and I share a common challenge; Grampy had difficulty learning with traditional teaching methods — and so do I. I was either born with or developed, a short-term memory impairment at a very young age. Perhaps it happened when a farm-hand coaxed me to jump out from the hayloft. He promised to catch me but didn't. Possibly Grampy and I had the same impairment; perhaps it is hereditary — no one knows.

In school during the mid-1950s to late 1960s, there was no help for my disability. If you looked normal, everything was normal. When it came to my studies, my mother attributed my problems to laziness. When I discovered my grandfather's learning issues, it surprised me that my mother didn't have more sympathy for my problems — not even after my diagnosis.

Long after Mom died, my father admitted to me that he had known there was something wrong. I asked Dad when he realized this, and he told me he'd tried to help me with my spelling words one evening. Dad said he would go over the spelling of one word, then move on to the next. When he returned to the first word, however, I couldn't spell it. Dad said he thought it was bad behavior at first, but his frustration disappeared when he realized there was more to my learning challenges than he could explain. There is much I don't remember about my childhood, but I do recall that last time Dad helped me with my spelling. I'm not sure why something wasn't done about this issue when I was a child. I wish I had asked my father that question.

As an adult, I learned techniques to manage in a world that caters to the 'normal.' I did want to be a teacher but by the time I realized I could, it was almost impossible to find teaching positions in Canada — so this wasn't practical anymore. I believe I would have made a great teacher because of my impairment and my personal experiences.

Now that I'm in my senior years, most of my family and friends complain about their poor memories. I often laugh to myself. More than ever before, I fit in with my peers. I'm finally at a stage in life where it is acceptable to fail to recall a name, place, or event! There are no more looks of confusion. Now, the only response to my memory loss is a nod of understanding.

Chapter 7

# Max

> During the First World War, my father served in the German Army. Don't worry - his soldiering did not help the Germans much.
>
> -VERA OLGA (NAFTHAL) GOLDSTON

**Before WWI, the region** of Memelland in Lithuania was appropriated by Prussia, a German state since 1871. As a result, Lithuanians living in Memelland automatically became German citizens.

In 1914, the Germans imposed a law drafting the young men of Memelland into the German army. This meant that Lithuanian soldiers were expected to fight against their countrymen. These were difficult times because good friends and family members were forced to fight on opposite sides.

When WWI began on July 28, 1914, eighteen-year-old Max received his orders to enlist and serve in the German army. He was not a fighter and considered himself a Lithuanian. Jews and Gentiles alike did not want to wage war against their own citizens. Most of the Memelland army consisted of unwilling soldiers. This was especially true for its Jewish soldiers, including Max.

Max's soldiering did not help the Germans, and for that — he felt only relief. Max quickly became a prisoner of war and was sent to Turkey or Servia[26] for the remainder of the conflict.

In due time Max got into a heated disagreement with another soldier. The soldier became so angry, that he pushed Max into the outdoor latrine. Max fell backward into the waste and was completely traumatized by the experience.

Finally, on November 11, 1918, WWI came to an end. The defeated Germans were forced to return Memelland to their rightful owner — the country of Lithuania. For years the Germans proclaimed they lost WWI because they were stabbed in the back by the Jews of Memelland.

Twenty-two year old Max was released from prison, returned to Memel and reunited with his family. He was thrilled to be home, but he made the mistake of telling his brothers about his one memorable event in the German army, which ended with him up to his ears in the latrine. He expected sympathy from his brothers. Instead, there was a moment of silence at the end of his story, and then the laughter and jokes began. The story would continue to haunt Max as good family humour for decades.

At the end of the war, Max's father Wolfe retired from his lumber business. His two elder sons, Nathan and Bernard, created a partnership and took over the family business renaming it N. Nafthal & Co. Later, Bernard left the business and moved his family to Germany.

During the post-war years, many business opportunities emerged for Max. In the early 1920s, he established his own brokerage company for wood and timber, *Nafthal ir Ko* (Nafthal and Co.). It was a great success, and Max was able to build an impressive house in Memel. Once the large house was built, he needed a wife and children to complete the picture.

Chapter 8

# Liza and Max

> Mutti [Mother; Liza] was a poor refugee girl with a well-known Jewish background and weak lungs from slow starvation after the Revolution. But very pretty with a good figure, just like what good old Max would go for. Vati [Daddy; Max] had a very large house; he was very wealthy at the time. Although stout and bald, he was quite the debonair young gent. Always dressed to the nines and very generous with one and all, and liked the good life. I wouldn't be surprised if a schatchen - marriage broker - was used to make the match for Mutti for that reason. How else would they have crossed paths?
>
> -VERA OLGA (NAFTHAL) GOLDSTON

Liza and her brother, Grisha, spent the remainder of the Great War in London with their older sister and brother-in-law. But Liza never talked about her life in England — and that was that.

During WWI, the Jews suffered from such profound prejudice that their powerful resources were completely depleted. In Russia, the Jews lost their ability to influence business dealings throughout

Europe. By 1919, the Soviet government began arresting innocent Russian Jews, including the Rabbis. Jewish properties were seized, communities were dissolved, and Jews were banned from teaching English in their schools.

There was nothing left in Russia for the Isserlin siblings; their properties, money and deep-seated roots were gone. During those dangerous times, Russian Jews began to rebuild their lives from nothing — but this did not interest Liza. She never returned to Russia, although she did return to Europe.

Sometime after the war, Liza's brother-in-law Kolia took a transfer with the Thomas Hedley Soap & Candle Company in England and moved his family to Wilna, Poland. Grisha also returned to Europe and settled in Warsaw, Poland. He established himself as a successful merchant like his father and married a beautiful woman named Aniela. In the early 1920s, Liza was in Zoppot[27] — a town on the Baltic Sea in northern Poland. The family was very happy to be back in Europe, although this would prove to be a fatal mistake.

In the years following the Great War, a recession plagued Europe. Soldiers returned home looking for available work, which left women with few employment opportunities. Even in good times, job openings for well-educated young women like Liza simply did not exist. Wealthy young girls were not brought up to find employment. But there was one opportunity open to her. She was bright, ambitious, independent, and raised to marry well. Why should the Great War stop her?

Liza continued to suffer serious gut and lung issues as a result of her near starvation. Although penniless and in poor health, she still had much to offer. Liza decided it was time to secure that good marriage.

During this era, it was essential for a young woman to have a bridal dowry. Though Liza had no monetary wealth, she had plenty of assets to help secure an excellent marriage. Her list of attributes was short but powerful — the Isserlin family name was recognized throughout Europe. Liza had a proper education and the training required to manage a large household. She was also fluent in eight languages. Together, these attributes had considerable value, which would certainly benefit the right man. Liza's radiant beauty and terrific figure nicely completed her dowry package.

This was just what Max would go for — a beauty with a good figure, and the right family, breeding and education. He didn't care about money; he had more than enough to share.

In the early 1920s, Max stood proud and confident. He was also stout and bald, which suited him. He was quite the debonair young gent, a generous spender, and a popular bachelor with the ladies. Max's charisma lit up the room. He loved the good life and had the means to enjoy it. Max loved to travel, eat in the best restaurants, and stay in the finest hotels. He was quite the catch — and Liza was the girl who caught him.

The two met while Max was travelling in Zoppot for business. There are two versions of this meeting. According to Liza's account, the beautiful, fiery young Russian girls were very popular with all the men. "We could have the pick of the litter when it came to men. Max took one look at me and couldn't resist."

The other version of their meeting was more realistic. A *schatchen*, or Jewish matchmaker, introduced Liza to Max. Matchmakers were hired often in those days, especially among the Jewish population.

A courtship began, and the dynamic couple was soon making plans for their future. But as their love grew, the German economy spiraled from extreme prosperity to deep recession. Liza was fitted for and ordered her bridal dress, which cost a small fortune. By the time she received the wedding gown, the economy had plummeted to the point that her dress was almost worthless.

On April 19, 1923, Liza and Max were married in Zoppot, Poland. Max was twenty-seven and Liza was two years younger. Shortly after the wedding, Max proudly returned to Memel, Lithuania, with his beautiful bride.

---

It's unclear whether Liza lived in Wilna or Warsaw with her family — I only know she was in Zoppot, Poland, in the early 1920s. She might have lived there, or she might simply have been visiting friends or family.

Decades later, my mother had her own opinion of how her parents first met. "If not for a matchmaker, how else would their paths have crossed? After all, Mutti was a poor, sickly refugee girl, and Vati was a wealthy and successful businessman."

I'm not so sure as my mother. After all, my grandmother would not have been alone in Zoppot. Many people would have been honoured to provide an introduction between a beautiful Isserlin family member and a well-established, popular bachelor from the Nafthal family.

Chapter 9

# The Courting Is Over, the Marriage Begins

> Vati sent Mutti to Italy for six months to cure her lungs. He dressed her like a queen and bought her jewellery. They lived in the lap of luxury.
>
> ---
>
> Mutti spent six weeks waiting for the birthing event in Das Klinik Butterberg; no wonder I always had to fight a weight problem. With Mutti's infant daughter's silver spoon well lodged in her mouth, complete with a well-trained nurse, she officially immigrated me to Memel, the luxurious home, and the good life.
>
> -VERA OLGA (NAFTHAL) GOLDSTON

**Shortly after their marriage,** Max sent Liza to Italy for six months to cure her lungs of the effects of near starvation. The expensive treatments were successful, and Liza never complained about her lungs again.

Max loved treating Liza like a queen and showing her off to friends and family. He took great pride in Liza's beauty, showering her with fashionable clothes, expensive jewelry and first-class travel. In return, Liza managed their home beautifully. She treated their servants with compassion and their guests with generosity. She hosted extravagant dinners and parties — always extending warm hospitality to guests, whether they were visiting for an evening or weeks. The family lived in the lap of luxury and were always happy to include other people in their good fortune.

Liza fit Max's ideal perfectly — a beautiful wife, with a proper upbringing. She looked stunning on his arm which meant everything to Max. Liza benefited from the marriage as well. She had returned to the grand lifestyle of her childhood, and she thrived with Max's lavish pampering.

In 1925, as Liza and Max were enjoying all the luxuries of their new life together, Adolf Hitler published his first book, a racist manifesto called *Mein Kampf* (My Struggle). In his writing, Hitler referred to the Jews as "parasites." The book was filled with grammatical errors, revealing that Hitler was not a scholar. Initially the work had limited success, however, it would eventually become the bible of Nazism in Germany's Third Reich. No Jews paid attention to these writings. Liza and Max's life continued with a focus on their exciting news.

Shortly after their second wedding anniversary on May 28, 1926, Liza and Max welcomed their first and only child into the world — Vera Olga Nafthal. As was common practice for the wealthy, Liza spent six weeks waiting for the birth in *Das Klinik Butterberg*, (Butter Mountain Clinic), in Königsberg, Germany. After Vera's birth, Liza spent another six weeks convalescing at the clinic.

The Ashkenazi Jewish custom is to give a newborn the name of a deceased family member. In receiving the name of a beloved relative, the child will adopt the virtues of their namesakes. It is believed, the loved one's soul will live on in the child who bears their name. Vera's middle name, Olga, honoured Liza's mother, Olga Isserlin. Grandmother Olga died during the Russian Revolution after contracting Typhus Fever, and Liza kept her mother's memory alive through her daughter.

---

Mom was fluent in five different languages. My grandmother in many more, however, I only heard them speak English. The exception was that Mom called her parents Mutti and Vati, German names for mother and father. Sometimes Vera used the Yiddish words meaning incompetent person or fool — *schlemiel* or *schmuck*.

When my mother married and started a family of her own, she was very firm about her children fitting in. This was likely the result of her experience of hatred and exclusion in her native country. Mom's childhood horrors influenced how she raised her own family. She had tolerance only for what she believed to be 'normal.' Speaking many languages in rural Nova Scotia wouldn't be considered normal. Another concern of my mother in speaking different languages would have been her husband, my father. Dad was born and raised in London, England, a true cockney who only spoke English.

As a child, I didn't think about this. But as an adult reflecting, I'm surprised that I never walked in on a private conversation to overhear Mom and Nanny speaking any other language.

Chapter 10

# The City of Memel

> My mother did the shopping, helped look after me, and visited and went to teas. She travelled a lot and generally took me along in the summer to Paris, Zoppot, Danzig and Czechoslovakia.
>
> -VERA OLGA (NAFTHAL) GOLDSTON

**Memel's greatest asset is** its geographical location, Lithuania's only port of entry to the Baltic Sea. This resulted in significant financial opportunities. Wealthy Jews came from all corners of Lithuania to establish new factories and businesses: flax exports, fertilizer imports, the timber trade, wool and cotton textile industries, as well as the import/export of food products. In addition, tobacco processing from Lithuanian growers was thriving. Prospects for well-paid, secure employment improved, which boosted Memel's overall economy. All sectors benefited: the arts, retail stores, exclusive hotels and expensive restaurants. The city catered to everyone's tastes.

After WWI, anti-Semitic restrictions disappeared for many years. The comfortable German lifestyle of pre-war times returned and was prevalent in Memel. The most prominent spoken language continued to be German. Max and Liza loved the vibrant city.

The couple built a good marriage together because that is what one did. As a bachelor, Max had been very popular among the ladies. His popularity continued even after the wedding, and he still loved the attention of beautiful women. Sometimes Liza would wonder about this, but she was never overly concerned. She had suffered so many losses by the time she met Max, that romance and passion were not of great importance to her. She was Max's cherished wife, and she was happy with that.

Most of Liza's time was taken up maintaining a happy, comfortable home for her family. Liza also loved to travel, visiting family and friends throughout Europe. If Vera had a school holiday, she joined her mother. Otherwise, Vera would stay home with her nurse. Max's time was consumed by business. The couple didn't spend all their days together, nor did they question each other's activities. Together or not, life was full and busy for the dynamic husband and wife.

Managing the Nafthal household and caring for Vera kept Liza busy. Along with a full-time cook and nurse, the family employed daily housemaids and a laundress who came in every week. A seamstress came in several times a year to sew clothing and do the mending.

Since Liza did not know how to drive and Max seldom drove himself, the Nafthals also employed a full-time chauffeur. As the lady of the house, Liza maintained good relationships with the staff and kept the household operating efficiently. She took over the household's bookkeeping, planned extravagant dinners and parties, and managed their ever-demanding social calendar.

While Max loved to eat, Liza knew nothing about cooking. She knew nothing about the workings of a kitchen. Liza did understand shopping in open-air markets for the best food for her beautifully arranged table.

Fresh eggs, produce, and dairy arrived at the Nafthal's back door from the rural farms each morning. Other delicacies came from the vibrant fish market. Fishmongers stood at long tables, calling out the daily catch; "Live fish for sale!"[28] Customers would rush forward before the freshest fish disappeared, but the fishmonger would keep his eye out for Liza, knowing the Nafthal household purchased only the best — and plenty of it. When Liza appeared, he would call out to her to come forward. Liza never stood in lineups for anything. She chose her fish quickly, then the monger would kill, gut, fillet, and wrap her purchases.

At the meat market, a huge variety of meats and smoked sausages were available. A live chicken was chosen, then beheaded, feathered, gutted and wrapped by the butcher, ready for the kitchen.[29] In the afternoon, the cook rubbed the bird with freshly-churned butter and herbs, and it was roasted in the oven with farm vegetables — all ready to be served in the dining room that evening.

Although the cook was also an excellent baker, Memel was renowned for its wonderful bakeries. These shops were located on every street corner, filling the air with the irresistible fragrance of German loaves of bread and rich European pastries.[30]

There was never a shortage of gourmet meals at the Nafthal table, and their guests enjoyed every mouthful. In return for their hospitality, the couple received many invitations to social events and travel opportunities. Although Liza had suffered many losses in her life, she was still able to enjoy her good fortune, and so she settled happily into her role as wife and mother.

---

A well-laden table and guests were prominent throughout my childhood, and I continued the tradition with my own family and friends. My philosophy regarding hospitality comes from my mother and grandmother — home and food are meant to be shared with family and friends. Cooking and baking from scratch are skills I use to express my lifestyle and my love. To this day, food continues to play an important role in how my family expresses themselves. Our home has an open-door policy — everyone is welcome.

Chapter 11

# The Curonian Spit Vacations

> Vati sang at the top of his lungs as we traveled through the woods and along the sand dunes to the Moose Reserve. Once there Vati's singing stopped, so as not to disturb the moose in their natural habitat. The moose often wandered the public beaches, with no one paying much attention to them. The children continued to play, and the moose didn't interrupt whatever important things they were doing. Often the moose walked into the sea, and once over their heads, they'd swim so far out, they would turn into specks on the water.
>
> These times had never been a happier, or better life, that a child could have had.
>
> -VERA OLGA (NAFTHAL) GOLDSTON

**The Nafthal family spent** most of their summers and special holidays on the Curonian Spit on the Baltic Sea. Max's father, Wolfe, owned a beautiful cottage in the village of Schwartzort. All the Nafthals loved to get away from the hectic city and visit the peninsula's cottage country. This meant grandparents, many aunts, uncles and cousins, with Vera being the youngest of the family all gathered in the summer months and during holidays. Vera adored her large family, especially Opapa, her grandfather Wolfe.

The Curonian Spit is a long, narrow stretch of land attached to East Prussia at the south end, and open to the sea at the Port of Memel. This created a busy canal, filled with many ships and small boats. The peninsula is only accessible by water from Lithuania. A ferry travelled back and forth from Memel's harbour to the peninsula, picking up and dropping off visitors.[31] On summer evenings a large steamship travelled from Germany to bring more visitors to the pier at the popular seaside community of Smiltyne.

Smiltyne bustled with restaurants, little shops and lemonade stands. Cafés were everywhere, and a violinist played in the streets just past the pier. A night market materialized every evening, and sellers' stands appeared with fresh fruit, cakes and candy.[32] Vera loved it.

Beyond the pier, a walking trail led through a magical pine forest. The path opened to a viewpoint overlooking a spectacular white sandy beach. The panoramic view of the Baltic Sea was stunning, with its scattered dunes and seagrasses blowing in the light ocean breeze. Hundreds of brightly coloured cabanas sat in straight rows along the shoreline. The clear blue waters glistened in the sun. All of this created a haven for sunbathers, swimmers and families. The peninsula offered a charming holiday resort for wealthy Lithuanians and Germans alike, including Jewish families from both countries.[33] Gentiles and Jews happily socialized together, and the Nafthal family loved their holidays in the cottage country.

Sometimes the family took Wolfe's horse and buggy for a day's tour along the beaches and across the peninsula. Max sang at the top of his lungs as they traveled through the woods and along the sand dunes to the Moose Reserve. Once they arrived, Max's singing stopped so the moose wouldn't be disturbed in their natural habitat.

No one paid much attention to the moose as the animals wandered the public beaches. Children continued playing, and the moose did not interrupt their important games. Often the moose would walk out into the sea. Once over their heads, these amazing creatures would swim until they were barely visible.

In addition to the moose, there were other treasures along the shore. The white sandy beaches of the Baltic Sea are known worldwide for their exquisite amber — and Vera and her Nafthal cousins spent hours searching for chunks of these precious gems. Liza loved to sit and watch the children randomly picking up a piece here and there. Vera was very serious about the quality of her private collection. Authentic amber carried static properties. Vera would retrieve a tin box holding bits of paper from the front of her swimsuit, then rapidly rub each chunk over her cotton bathing suit to test her specimens. Holding the charged stone over the paper, she would stand very still and hold her breath. If the gem lifted the paper, it was genuine amber, and Vera would let out a loud yell. Holding her prize tightly with both hands, she'd run as fast as her legs would carry her, dropping the chunk on her mother's lap for safekeeping. Vera would give a huge huff if it was not genuine, toss the chunk away, and pick up another.

Vera's large amber collection was one of her most prized possessions, and she proudly displayed it in her bedroom. When Nazi persecution eventually forced the family to flee Lithuania, the amber collection was left behind. Vera was devastated.

---

I think about my mother's childhood memories of the magnificent moose. These huge beasts have never ceased to amaze me — massive and oddly shaped, yet graceful in their light-footed movements. Moose have always been my favourite wild animals. Mom once gave me a beautiful wooden brooch in the shape of a moose for my winter coat, but she never said a word about the Moose Reserve that she remembered so fondly from her childhood. To this day, the little wooden moose still has a function. I pinned it to the red toque that I knit my husband years ago. Each Christmas season, the old toque and its wooden moose top our festive tree.

I continue to be astonished at my mother's silence. There were so many connections between our lives together and Mom's life as a child, but she never shared them. If Mom hadn't left behind those few pages, I would never have known about the moose.

---

The first time I learned about Mom's amber collection was in the same few pages, that she wrote shortly before her death. The gems must have been very important to have appeared in these pages, and that surprises me. My sister Peggy and I were both born in November and we are Scorpios with amber colored birthstones — topaz. When I was a child, Mom gave me an amber ring for a special occasion. Knowing my mother, she would have vigorously rubbed that amber ring on her cotton dress, then held bits of paper over it to test its authenticity. I'm certain she couldn't have resisted.

I don't believe Mom intended to take me on such an emotional journey when she wrote those few last pages. Still, I cannot explain the grief my discoveries have caused me over the past several years.

## Chapter 12

# Max: The Big Shot!

> Vati was always the big pal, the big spender. The Big Shot signed a note for a German friend in Heidelberg. The pal went broke and took Mutti and Vati with him.
>
> -VERA OLGA (NAFTHAL) GOLDSTON

**Max loved to be** the big shot with everyone. He was always the big pal, the big spender — and sometimes this got him into trouble.

In contrast to Liza, who trusted no one unless they proved themselves, Max trusted everyone and believed that nothing bad could ever happen to him. His trusting nature led to financial devastation for the family. Much later, it could have cost the family their lives.

Sometime around 1928, Max signed a note for a German friend in Heidelberg. But the pal went broke and took Max and Liza down with him. The timber business, luxurious home, valuables and money were all confiscated; everything was lost. Hard times hit the couple badly, and Max was forced to face his father. Thankfully, Wolfe took pity on his son and generously invited them into the Nafthal family home in Memel. They quickly accepted.

Vera was only two years old. On a positive note, Wolfe and Vera adored each other, and they were happy to be together. As the baby of his grandchildren, Wolfe spoiled her terribly. So far as Vera was concerned, the silver spoon with which she'd been born stayed firmly lodged in her mouth.

While Wolfe provided the family with a roof over their heads and food to eat, Max was expected to get back into business on his own. Liza and Max asked for nothing else. When their shoes had holes, they lined them with linoleum. In 1929, the stock market crashed, but Max had expertise in the timber business, as well as the right friends and professional connections. Their penny-pinching was only necessary for a short time. It wasn't long before his business was up and running again.

Within a few years, Max bounced back from his financial difficulties. The family moved from Wolfe's home to a rented apartment in a nice neighbourhood on Bahnhof Strasse (Station Street). The good life was back again.

Max worked long hours and made many friends and professional acquaintances as he travelled for business to England, Russia, Poland, Sweden, Holland and Germany. His efforts paid off big time. Liza managed their new home and helped the nurse take care of Vera. Shopping began again. They resumed entertaining, and their social calendar was busy once more.

Max's business continued to grow and the family moved again, this time to a luxurious new apartment. They were one of the few families in Memel to own a refrigerator, radios, record players and a vehicle. Life was grand.

Liza resumed the travel she loved. She visited family and friends in Paris, Czechoslovakia, and Sopot and Danzig in the Polish Corridor. Vera stayed home with her nurse through the school terms, but during summer vacations and holidays — when they weren't on the peninsula — she toured with her mother. The little girl loved spending time with her large family and their many friends throughout Europe.

Vera's favourite Isserlin relative was a cousin named Eva Kirschner (Cyrinski), who was thirteen years older than Vera. Vera also adored Eva's mother, Eugenia (Isserlin), and Julia Cukierman (Lypnik) who was Eva's older half-sister on her mother's side. People were drawn to the three women's beauty — both inside and out — and especially to Eva. The family only spoke Russian at home, and the three ladies loved to spoil Vera when she visited. Liza also adored Eva, and throughout her lifetime often spoke about how much she missed her.

The family had a home in Vilna, Lithuania, where Eva was born, and also a villa in Sopot, Poland, on the coast of the Baltic Sea, and two houses in Danzig. The family also lived in Warsaw for a time and later purchased a lovely flat in Paris. Liza and Vera could have stayed in any one of these homes, perhaps in all of them, but, likely, Vera's visits were mainly in Danzig and Paris.[34]

Max somtimes joined his wife and daughter in Danzig and Paris. Vera said these were her favourite holidays because her father was with them. Normally, his life in Memel was so consumed with his business that he had little time left for Vera. Liza's family spoke Russian and French, but Max did not understand either language, and so on these trips, he gave his undivided attention to his daughter. Vera loved this attention, and so did Max! He would place his daughter on his lap and say, "Well, at least you'll never speak Russian or French so your poor Vati can't understand, will you, Veraushka?" The term of endearment '*ushka*' was Max's only Russian achievement, and he used it sparingly only with Liza and Vera.

Vera laughed when her father said such things, then looked crossly at her mother for speaking a language her father did not understand. In those days, it was not unusual for Europeans to speak many languages. Vera was fluent in Russian and French, but she preferred to spend this special time with her father. The unusual thing was that Max never learned these languages.

---

Sometimes my grandfather called Vera *Veraushka* and Liza *Lizaushka* as terms of endearment. He was proud of this because *ushka* was the only word he knew in Russian. What he might not have known is that *ushka* means 'old woman!' I wonder if my mother was mistaken in her writings, or if my grandmother was having a bit of fun at my grandfather's expense.

---

Vera's favourite cousin, Eva, had a brother named Monia. He had been living in Palestine since before WWII. When the family realized Europe would not be safe for Jews, he wanted to bring them all to Palestine. To enter the country, however, they needed certificates from Palestine's British rulers. These certificates were difficult to obtain and came with a heavy price tag. He eventually obtained the paperwork they needed, and in March 1940, Eva and her mother, Eugenia, boarded the last boat to leave Marseilles, France, during wartime. On April 1, 1940, they docked safely in Haifa, Palestine, where they met up with Monia.

Eva's half-sister, Julia, her husband Joseph Cukierman, and son Alexander (Alex) remained in France. Julia and Alex survived, however Joseph came to a mysterious death.[35] There is more information about Julia, Joseph and Alex's story to come.

---

Liza never visited her siblings because they left England and moved to Poland. The political turmoil led to harsh border restrictions that made travelling between the Union of Soviet Socialist Republics (USSR) and Lithuania difficult. For this reason, Vera never met her mother's siblings and their families. I do have a picture, however, of Grisha and his wife, Aniela, with the Nafthal brothers. The whereabouts of the family gathering and the date is unknown.

Chapter 13

# Political Turmoil in Germany

> So things were great, but clouds were forming over Germany. Although for a long time was contained to Germany alone, our nice, comfortable, happy times were beginning to cloud over.
>
> -VERA OLGA (NAFTHAL) GOLDSTON

THE MEMEL JEWS RECEIVED the first reports of growing anti-Semitism in the German Reich from neighbouring East Prussia. In 1933, East Prussian students were expelled from the University of Königsberg because they were Jews. They arrived in Memel as refugees, astonishing the community.

On January 30, 1933, Adolf Hitler became the new German Chancellor. Hitler was focused on his own anti-Semitic goals from the very beginning. Shortly after the election, Hitler secretly began to recruit his top officers into the established Nazi Party. He knowingly selected men capable of inflicting punishment on innocent citizens. Within a short period, the Nazi Party would grow into a mass dictatorial movement.

During this period, Max often travelled to Germany for business. He was still safe since only German Jews were targeted initially. When he returned to Memel, he always brought news of heated political matters. German radio reported some but not all of the Nazi anti-Semitism directed toward German Jews. In the beginning, anti-Semitic demonstrations only occurred in Germany. Most Lithuanian Jewish citizens did not feel personally threatened; this included Max and most other Europeans. Liza's instincts made her believe the opposite — all European Jews should feel threatened by this madman.

On February 28, 1933, less than two months after Hitler's appointment, the German government suspended the right to free speech, as well as freedom of assembly and the press, and freedom from invasion — measures which extended to mail, telephone and telegraph communication. The news coming out of Germany was limited to what the Nazis wanted others to know and hear. Soon the government authorized house searches without reasons or warrants.

On March 9, there were attacks against German Jews by the SA Sturmabteilung (Assault Division of the Army). The extremely violent SA were later well-known as the Brownshirts.

On March 20, the first concentration camp in Germany was established at Dachau. Three days later, on March 23, the Enabling Act was passed, allowing Hitler to introduce new laws without interference from the German president for the next four years. This was accomplished under intimidation from Hitler's growing Nazi Party.

On April 1, the Nazi Party organized a boycott of Jewish-owned businesses and Jewish professionals throughout Germany. The Nazis used intimidation and threats as they stood guard outside stores and offices, holding signs and shouting such slogans as; "don't buy from Jews," and "the Jews are our misfortune." This lasted one day, and Germans continued to shop and seek services from Jewish businesses and professionals.

"What of all this?" Liza asked her husband just before he left for another business trip. She showed him the headlines in the newspaper.

Max kissed his wife on the cheek. "The Jews have been persecuted for years. It will be alright," he promised, as he rushed out the door.

By April 7, Jewish citizens were barred from working in the civil service. Initially, Jewish WWI veterans, and Jews who lost fathers and sons during the war were exceptions. But that soon changed.

German Jewish lives became more difficult with the introduction of a new law on April 25. The 'Law against Overcrowding in Schools and Universities' limited the number of Jewish students in public schools.

Just a day later, on April 26, the Gestapo was created. Also known as the German Secret Police or the SS, the Gestapo was capable of extreme violence toward innocent people.

Nazis' infamous political police force was now in motion. The Gestapo's purpose was to enforce Nazism's most radical ideas and goals using ruthless intimidation, brutal interrogations, and violent torture. Their brutality increased as Hitler's power grew.

"The Gestapo! Who are these people?" cried Liza.

"Hitler's thugs; they'll all be stopped," Max said, though he could see his wife was worried.

On May 7, the German government fired Jewish workers from all civil service positions. With support from the Nazi Party, a

German student organization led anti-Jewish rallies across Germany on May 10. To 'purify' German libraries, all books written by Jews, political opponents and liberal intellectuals were burned.

On July 14, Germany proclaimed itself a one-party state. The Nazi Party, headed by Adolf Hitler, became the sole legal political party in Germany. Hitler's power over the country was complete; he answered to no one.

One evening, while Liza knitted a sweater for Vera, she listened to a German news report on the radio. "Max, this Adolf Hitler is big trouble for the Jews!"

Max looked up from his newspaper and smiled at his beautiful, young wife. "Nonsense. Germany will take care of this foolishness quickly."

Liza was shocked at her husband's response. She frowned and continued staring at Max long after his attention had returned to his newspaper.

On September 17, German-Jewish organizations were established to represent the interests of Jews throughout Germany. In truth, they were powerless against the Nazis.

Days later, on September 22, German newspapers and radio announced that the newly founded Chambers of Literature, Press, Broadcasting, Theatre, Film, Music and Fine Arts were all denying membership to Jews. This meant that all Jewish citizens were excluded from employment in the cultural sector.

On September 29, the 'Hereditary Farm Law' was enacted. It specified that farms could only be inherited by German farmers who could prove they had no Jewish or coloured[36] ancestors dating back to January 1, 1800. As a result, German Jews lost their farms to Nazi Germany.[37]

It was a devastating year for Jewish German citizens. Some had no choice but to leave their homeland and emigrate to other countries. Others wanted to leave but lacked the financial means to uproot their families and move them to a new country. These Jews were trapped. And for those who chose to stay in a European country, their protection would be short-lived. There were many German Jews of the same mindset as Max — the insanity had to be stopped.

But Liza was not convinced it would be stopped. "Max, I worry that this craziness in Germany will move throughout Europe!"

Max spread his arms wide. "Look at what we have here in Memel. We're safe; our lives are good. We're happy!"

Liza could only respond by shaking her head.

For now, Max had the last word. "This foolishness will come to an end. Wait and see."

The couple agreed on only one element concerning German politics — Hitler's first year in power had been appalling. As a result of their differing political opinions, the couple began to argue.

Not far in the distance, Liza could see dark clouds threatening their happy life.

Chapter 14

# Vera's School Days

> These were happy times.
>
> -VERA OLGA (NAFTHAL) GOLDSTON

**In 1930, the majority** of Memel citizens were either Jewish Lithuanians or non-Jewish Germans. In that year, five-year-old Vera started her formal education at Auguste-Viktoria Lyceum, a school for Jewish and Gentile girls. Vera loved school and all her friends and teachers.

By 1933-1934, however, the school's attitude had changed drastically. The reason for this attitude shift was simple — Nazis now lived in Memel.

German Nazis had no official authority in the city, but the Party's popularity was growing as a result of a large number of German citizens. These Germans listened to Nazi propaganda constantly, believing it would improve their lives. The Nazis began to interfere with the Memel policy experts, including matters of education.

The majority of teachers in Memel were German Lithuanians. This was not a politically motivated plan; it just happened that many German Lithuanians were interested in the teaching profession. Some of these teachers became Nazi sympathizers, hoping Memel would fall under the German Reich.

It became mandatory for German students to participate in a nationalist group. Although they were not Hitler Youth groups, they had similarities. German pupils were taught to march at a young age and to sing songs of the homeland. Memel's Jewish students were always excused.

Vera and her friends did not care that they were left out. They had no interest in wasting their time marching back and forth going nowhere. Since Vera was never able to carry a tune, the singing was of no interest to her. Instead, Vera continued to enjoy her studies and books. Her teachers were kind and she was a popular student with many close Jewish friends. She remained a happy girl.

Chapter 15

# The Nazis in Memel

> Refugees from Germany, then from Austria, then from Czechoslovakia started to come to Lithuania and stay only long enough to get visas to the United States of America (U.S.A.), Canada and Australia - anywhere away from the European continent. We entertained and kept many refugees as our guests. And of course I heard first hand the many stories - which later became so familiar - of the very beginning of the time which was to become the Holocaust, and from which we were lucky to escape.
>
> -VERA OLGA (NAFTHAL) GOLDSTON

**Liza continued listening to** disturbing radio broadcasts, which described one violent event after another. Adolf Hitler's loathsome hatred, brutal violence and appetite for world power were growing daily. He was now setting his sights on other parts of Europe.

On August 2, 1934, Germany's political situation deteriorated even more when Adolf Hitler became President and Chancellor of the country.[38] Hitler immediately abolished the President's office and declared himself Führer of the German Reich and People.

On August 19, Adolf Hitler was declared the absolute dictator of Germany, placing him above the state and its laws.

By 1934, the city of Memel and its Jewish citizens began to feel the effects of the trouble in Germany. The first shocking display of swastikas and propaganda banners had begun to appear on walls and windows of some of Memel's Jewish businesses. At the same time, the German Consulate in Memel started to harass Jewish citizens.[39]

Max's brother, Nathan Nafthal was a well-respected businessman and owner of the timber mill N. Nafthal & Co. He was also vice-president of the Memel Chamber of Commerce and an active citizen of the city. When Nathan applied through the Consulate to the German Reich for a multiple-entry visa to Germany, he was only issued a single-entry visa.[40] This meant he'd lost his privileges to travel freely back and forth across the German border.

At the same time, the Gestapo began monitoring Nathan's every move.[41] Nathan had good reason to be worried for himself, his wife Helene, and their children, Ursula and Alfred. His third child, the eldest daughter Hilde (Nafthal) Sturmann, was safe in Palestine.

In 1935, many ethnic Memelland Germans were members of the National Socialist German Workers' Party (the official name of the Nazi Party). The Memelland National Socialist and other Lithuanian newspapers supported the German Reich. They declared that they were 'victims of a Jewish conspiracy,' since Jewish judges and Jewish state attorneys participated in criminal cases against the Party.[42]

By March 16, 1935, Hitler's army exceeded the restricted number of soldiers allowed by the Treaty of Versailles. The treaty had been signed at the end of WWI, defining peace terms between the victorious Allies and defeated Germans. The treaty held Germany responsible for starting the first world war and included harsh penalties which Hitler used to fuel events leading up to WWII.

On September 15, 1935, Nazi Germany's Nuremberg Laws came into effect. The laws established a framework for the anti-Semitic principles which were the foundation of Nazi ideology — a belief in German privilege and the dehumanization of Jews. These racist laws outraged Memel's Jewish population.[43]

The Nuremberg Laws hit too close to home for Liza. Among them was a law against 'Race-Mixing,' stating that marriages and extramarital relationships between Jews and Gentiles were forbidden and punishable by death. This punishment applied to the Jew, the non-Jew, and any offspring of the couple. Max's younger brother Felix was a rebel who wouldn't listen to anyone. He was involved with a Gentile girl named Charlotte (Lottie), and both were young and stubborn to a fault. Under normal circumstances, Liza wouldn't have cared who Felix was dating, however, the Nazi ideology frightened her. If Germany seized Memelland, Liza was afraid the two lovebirds would bring attention to themselves and the Nafthal family with potentially deadly consequences. But though her fears were justified, Liza had other matters to worry about.

Liza was convinced that what was happening in Germany could spread throughout Europe. They were far too close to the trouble. In Germany, it was public knowledge that many Jews were removed from society, brutally intimidated and cruelly beaten. The Nazis stopped people on the streets based on their outward appearance, demanding to know if they were Jewish. Vera's features did not match the Nazi ideal. Liza looked at her daughter and shivered — she had dark olive skin, black hair and chocolate brown eyes. How she wished Vera looked more like her, with fair skin, light-coloured hair and soft brown eyes. A lighter complexion was so much safer in these times.

Max, like most Jews, continued to believe these ideas were ludicrous and would eventually be condemned by the authorities. After all, insane men can't rule a country or push their fierce influence onto other nations. He was so wrong.

In the fall of 1935, German authorities prohibited traders from travelling to Memel's annual market. Memel began rethinking their relationship with Germany.

In 1936, many Jewish stores and businesses closed their doors in protest during Yom Kippur and Rosh Hashanah,[44] something which had never happened before in the city. Many Jews prepared to leave Memel, by contacting relatives, friends, and professional associates in Germany, Latvia, Lithuania, and beyond.[45]

At the beginning of 1937, even more Nazis infiltrated Memel. The Lithuanian authorities refused to allow them to wear uniforms or march in public, and so anything to do with the Nazis was kept underground. But while they weren't recognized publicly, the Nazis did influence many city councillors and other Germans in powerful positions.

On February 26, 1937, the Memel City Council passed a law restricting the professional practice of Jewish judges.[46] Max's youngest brother, Sally, was a successful public prosecutor in Memel. The city council fired Sally because he was a Jew. To add to the insult, Sally was forbidden to practice law. He was single and so did not have the worry of a family to support, but he felt personally threatened by the Memel Germans and Nazis. He began travelling from one European country to another, hoping to avoid any further trouble with the Germans. He would have liked to travel to Hanover, Germany, where his brother Bernard lived, but it was too dangerous.

Max's only sister, Hanna Wolfsohn, and her husband, David were fortunately living in Kaunas, Lithuania. In 1936, the Nazis were not interested in all of Lithuania — their only interest was Memel for its valuable harbour on the Baltic Sea. The city of Kaunas still did not have a Nazi presence, which meant that the citizens were able to live comfortable lives free of Nazi Germany's influence.

Max pushed back initially when Liza insisted that he must stop travelling to Germany for business. He had never claimed to be a hero, so in the end, he agreed to stop travelling to Germany until the horrific political events blew over.

In the summer of 1937, German youths attacked young Jewish vacationers in the village of Schwarzort, where the Nafthals had their family summer home. This sent shockwaves through Memel's Jewish community. During the same year, ten Jewish students were assaulted by German Lithuanian students in two different secondary schools.[47] As Liza took note of these events, she could see the Nazis' influence spreading.

Liza listened to the news on the radio broadcasting one heartless event after another. Hitler was now setting his sights on other regions of Europe. On September 30, 1938, Germany took over Czechoslovakia; then Hitler turned his focus to his homeland, Austria. Germany had been forced to give up Austria after WWI, and Hitler wanted it back. He spent a great deal of time obsessing over this issue at his famous villa, the Berghof, near Berchtesgaden in the Bavarian Alps. The villa was well known for its great hall, which had a huge window that provided a panoramic view as far away as Austria. Hitler spent much of his time staring into the distance at the view — no matter what the cost, he was determined to reclaim his homeland.

On March 11, 1938, Nazi Germany seized Austria and immediately began a campaign of horrific cruelty toward Austrian Jews.

Jewish homes and businesses were looted and unlawfully seized. Jews were ostracized and no longer permitted to gather in public places. Jews were brutally imprisoned, tortured and sometimes murdered.

The madness and violence drove Jewish refugees from Austria and Czechoslovakia to Memel. In their attempt to flee Europe, many arrived at Liza and Max's front door for shelter. The refugees came with shocking stories of brutal treatment. No one yet realized that these crimes against Jews were the beginning of what would become the Holocaust.

A few refugees found countries to take them in. Many returned to their homes looking for family and were never seen again. Others remained in Lithuania since no other borders were open to them. The Jews who remained in Europe had a false hope of survival.

Liza and Max never turned anyone away. But even as they were sheltering refugees themselves, Liza began to formulate her plans to leave Lithuania and seek refuge outside of Europe. Max's persistent claim that this would all blow over upset Liza. She couldn't convince her husband that dangerous days were coming for the Memel Jews, and Max believed his wife was too consumed with political issues. In 1938, no one could have imagined the devastation that would result from Adolf Hitler's murderous hatred — not even Liza.

Liza was convinced there would soon be no way out of Europe. Fierce arguments continued between the couple, one wanting to stay, the other determined to leave. The political pressures and stress of constant fighting eventually led Liza and Max to live separate lives — although they both remained under the same roof.

At the breakfast table, Liza showed no interest in her meal as she listened to the latest news. "Max," she said, looking across the table at her husband. "We need to get out of here. We need to take Vera and leave Europe altogether!"

Max was so shocked at his wife's absurd idea, that his head shot up from his newspaper. "Nonsense — we will do no such thing! Germany will take care of these bullies. They'll be put in their place!"

"We will do what needs to be done to keep our daughter safe!" Liza insisted.

While Max heard his wife's words, he did not respond. He had never heard Liza use that tone of voice, and in truth — it shocked him.

Liza's commitment to leave Europe was intensifying, and her plans were becoming more concrete.

---

Many questions about the past have gone unanswered. I often wondered why my Great-Uncle Bernard and his family stayed in Hanover, Germany. The persecution started in 1933 and only got worse with each passing year. In truth, most German Jews didn't leave. Some could and didn't; others wanted to and couldn't. No matter the circumstances, it's very difficult to leave everything you know and love. This is another family mystery — one that will never have an answer.

Chapter 16

# Ostracized

**Sometime during 1938, many** of Vera's non-Jewish classmates and friends stopped acknowledging her — there was not even a wave or a slight glance her way. Others called her terrible names, like 'kike'[48] and 'rat.' They threatened her, shouting appalling statements such as; "the Gestapo is coming," and then ran away laughing. Vera was all too aware of the terrifying Gestapo.

Jews were now banned from restaurants, libraries, parks and all public places in Memel. Mutti and Vera no longer felt safe in their community. Vera knew most Germans hated her because she was Jewish, and that was frightening for such a young child. The good times were over — life had become scary.

Vera saw changes in Mutti's life as well. Her mother no longer attended teas, the theatre, or parties. Instead, mother and daughter stayed close to home, except when Mutti disappeared from time to time, without explanation. Vera always worried until Mutti was safely home again. She would have worried even more if she'd known her mother was smuggling money and valuables across the border.

Jewish families began to disappear from Memelland, some simply walking away from their homes and belongings. Wealthier Jews packed up their households and shipped their possessions to safer areas in Lithuania, or other European countries. The families followed their possessions — not realizing their safety would be short-lived.

It became clearer to Vera that no one could stop the disaster looming over their heads — not even her father, who had always been able to fix her silly childhood troubles. But Vera still had hope; she trusted Mutti.

---

My sister Peggy told me she noticed our mother's fearful response to a far-away siren once so asked our father about it. Dad said Mom was often startled at the distant ambulance or police sirens. These warnings always took her back to the frightening periods in her childhood. Imagine living with these horrifying feelings and nightmares for decades and never talking about it![49]

My grandmother was likely aware of Mom's fears as well, but I never knew. Mom never shared these feelings with me, nor did I ever notice signs of her fear. My mother was a great actress, and I believe my sister must have caught her at a vulnerable moment.

Peggy also admitted she had childhood nightmares of Gestapo boots stomping to the front door of our family home. She was afraid the Nazis were going to come and take us all away.[50] I felt a sadness for my sister when she confided this to me. I had never suffered from such nightmares, however, for decades I could not read about the Holocaust. It is true that my family's silence made me fearful of that period in history. The few times I tried to read a historical novel, it gave me terrifying anxiety that stayed with me for a long time. I wonder, "Are our fears one example that the first generation born after WWII were truly affected by the Holocaust?" I can not speak for my sister, but for me, I believe so.

Chapter 17

# The Doomed Evian Conference

> Franklin D. Roosevelt did nothing for the European Jews, and he could have.
>
> —VERA OLGA (NAFTHAL) GOLDSTON

**In early 1938, both** the United States (US) and the United Kingdom (UK) refused to accept any more European Jewish refugees. The US president, Franklin D. Roosevelt, assembled the Evian Conference in France from July 6-15, 1938. Thirty-two countries and two hundred international journalists participated, plus twenty-four volunteer organizations proposed plans to deal with the Jewish refugees.

The main discussion at the conference was the 'European refugee problem.' The number of European Jews fleeing persecution by the Nazis was increasing daily. Both Liza and Max hoped the world leaders would legislate an international plan for desperate European Jews. The US gained public attention when it enacted strict quotas on Jewish refugees entering America. Not wanting to address the ticking time bomb, Roosevelt avoided the refugee issue at the conference, and no decisions were made.[51]

Desperate Jews believed President Roosevelt and the US would be an important influence in their rescue, but the thirty-two countries at the conference were unable to reach an agreement. Liza was furious. In the wake of the disastrous Evian Conference, the European Jews were left without hope. The desperate situation became even clearer as all of Europe began to fall victim to Hitler and his Nazis.[52]

As Liza and Max continued their heated arguments, the attitudes of their non-Jewish neighbours and friends began to change. Nazi sympathizers appeared everywhere. It would only be a short time before Liza and Max were no longer safe in their own home.

Liza worried constantly. She could feel danger creeping ever closer to their front door. Max worried too, but like many other Jews, he still hoped the madness would be stopped.

The couple sat in silence at the dining room table one evening, Liza listening to the terrifying newscast on the radio, while Max read his paper.

"It's time to go, Max," said Liza.

"Where?"

"Anywhere away from the European continent."

Max slammed his fist on the table, harder than he meant. "Are you crazy? A strange country? My business is doing well! I won't be bullied into leaving my home and business by these insane Nazis!"

"If we don't leave, they'll kill us all," Liza said defiantly. She stood and stared down at her husband. A fist on the table did not frighten her.

Max heard her words and felt her cold gaze, but he did not look up from his paper again. Liza walked away; both knew the matter was far from over.

---

In my teen years, I developed a keen interest in history. But I stayed clear of WWII and the Holocaust. It was an unspoken agreement in our house — this era of history was not open for discussion. As a child, I was frightened by the silence that surrounded this subject — a past so terrible, that it was not talked about. Information wasn't as readily available in the 1950s and 60s as it is today, so the whole topic was easy to avoid.

I found a biography of Franklin D. Roosevelt in our local library. The world loved this president and his first lady, and I quickly came to adore Eleanor. Not far into the biography, I told Mom and Nanny about my great interest in the Roosevelts, thinking they'd be impressed. I'll never forget the look of shock and horror on their faces. Both hated Roosevelt. "He did nothing for the Jews in Europe, and he could have," they shouted in unison. That was the end of the conversation.

I was overwhelmed and ashamed. I felt I had betrayed my family. The lump in my throat stopped me from saying another word, and, instead, I accepted Mom and Nanny's horror without question. I felt the president and Eleanor had deceived me as if they were trying to lure me to their side. I rushed from the room before my tears flowed. My curiosity about Roosevelt ended at that moment; and I quickly returned the book to the library without reading another page. The subject was never mentioned again. I stopped talking about history altogether.

I can't help wondering today about the conversation that took place between Mom and Nanny after I ran from the room all those years ago.

The odd time, the president's name would come up in discussion among my friends and I was quick to say, "Roosevelt didn't help the European Jews during the Holocaust, and he could have." I received shocked silent stares from my friends. This only reinforced my belief that this era should never be talked about. Luckily for me, the subject didn't come up often — because I didn't have a clue what Roosevelt could have done for the Jews.

During my research into my family's history, I learned of the doomed Evian Conference. I finally understood Mom and Nanny's unexpected reaction that day. Instead of the botched conference being the Jewish salvation, it was used as a powerful tool for Nazi propaganda during the Holocaust. It was my turn to be completely horrified that one man had the power to help save millions of Jews from destruction — and did not. My mother and grandmother never got over Roosevelt's failure to act during the Evian Conference.

Decades later, I did discover that President Franklin D. Roosevelt eventually went against the counsel of his advisers and began to support Great Britain's war efforts. In mid-December 1940, Roosevelt created the Lend-Lease Act — the United States would lend — not sell — military supplies to Great Britain. Selling military supplies was prohibited, but lending was a way to get around the red tape. This also came with the conditions of leasing navel bases in the Caribbean and Newfoundland. The agreement came with the understanding that after the war America would be paid back. On December 31, 2006, Great Britain made its final payment toward the war loans. But for Mom and Nanny, the Lend-Lease Act came too late; so many had already been murdered. They could not get past their hatred of Roosevelt to see that some lives were saved with this legislation. I completely understand.

Chapter 18

# Vera's Nightmares

**Hitler and his Nazis** continued to make gains throughout Europe. On September 29, 1938, Germany, Italy, Great Britain and France signed the Munich Agreement, forcing Czechoslovakia to surrender the border region of the Sudetenland to Nazi Germany. There were three million Sudeten Germans living in the region, and Hitler was determined to unite all Germans into one nation. If his demand for the Sudetenland had not been met, Hitler threatened to unleash a European war. Germany terrified Europe, and for that reason, it motivated them to appease Hitler. Czechoslovakia was not included in the negotiations that saw the Sudetenland traded for a pledge of peace from Hitler, however, they agreed to the terms under pressure from Britain and France. Having conquered one land, Hitler quickly moved on to the next. His focus now turned to Memel, Lithuania.[53]

In the fall of 1938, the situation worsened for the Memel Jews. Germans posted more swastikas on Jewish businesses and prevented shoppers from entering Jewish stores. Memel Jews continued to emigrate to different regions in Lithuania and other countries — but no Jews in Europe were safe.

Liza and Max did their best to shelter Vera from the horrors inflicted on Jewish people.[54] But the thirteen-year-old knew plenty.

Being Jewish meant serious trouble for her whole extended family, including the children. Vera saw no apparent reason for this hatred.

No one noticed Vera listening to the adult conversations. She heard how the dangerous Nazis were sweeping across the continent. Now they'd arrived in her city, and she knew it.

Liza and Max harboured many displaced Austrian and Czech Jews in their home. All their stories carried a similar theme — they had fled their homeland to find refuge in Lithuania. Their properties had been confiscated, their bank accounts frozen, and they were forbidden to work. Many had also been beaten and tortured.

The families described the sound of Gestapo boots stomping to their doors, the soldiers banging and yelling for them to open up. The Nazis' wild dogs would bark and growl at the end of their chains. The dogs were kept hungry to make them more vicious. Families told of brutal violations in their homes, people heartlessly thrown out on the street, others arrested, and some shot dead where they stood. This included children of all ages, elderly grandparents and healthy aunts and uncles — whole families disappeared forever. Vera listened to these accounts over and over again.

The stories Vera and her girlfriends heard changed them forever and brought an end to the silly chit-chat of thirteen-year-olds. Instead, their conversations focused on the radical Adolf Hitler and the Nazis. The girls talked of nothing but the latest political events they overheard from the adults.

Liza tried to maintain some normalcy in her daughter's life. One evening, Vera attended a sleepover with several of her closest girlfriends. The conversation turned solemn the moment the grown-ups left the room. They shared their greatest worry — being trapped in a Jewish round-up by the Gestapo. After discussing the horrors of the Gestapo, the girls made a verbal pact — they would not allow themselves to be taken away. They would commit suicide before they could become victims of the Gestapo. Each girl explained how she would go about this. Vera's best friend said she would drown herself in the bathtub — and in the end, that is exactly what she did. Vera had a plan also, although her girlfriends were the only ones who knew what that plan was.

Not one friend survived the Holocaust.

---

Mom rarely talked about her childhood in Lithuania. I say 'rarely,' because she did break the silence on a few occasions. Without warning Mom would share a small piece of her history.

When I was about thirteen years old, I asked Mom's permission to host a sleepover for a few of my girlfriends. I knew the answer would be yes because Mom never said no to a houseful of people. There were always lots of friends in our family home, both adults and children.

Just as I predicted, Mom's yes came without hesitation. Right after the yes, however, a story poured out of Mom in her strong accent, well-known to the area of Memel.

"When I was about your age, I had sleepovers with my girlfriends too!"

Mom had my full attention. I asked what she did with her girlfriends during their sleepovers. Secretly, I was hoping for something different to do with my friends.

"We didn't play or talk about the same things you do with your friends," she continued.

I was hooked!

"At your age, my girlfriends and I would sit around in our nighties, eating our snacks and making pacts with each other."

"Pacts?" That sounded interesting.

"Yes, pacts."

"What kind of pacts?" I asked.

"Suicide pacts!"

I was stunned.

"We made promises that if the Nazis came for us at night, we would not go!"

"What would they do?" I asked, hoping my shock didn't show. By then, I knew cruel Nazis had ripped people from their homes, and those people had never returned.

"One of my closest girlfriends — such a pretty girl," Mom spoke without emotion. "She told us she would drown herself in her bathtub before the Nazis could take her away."

"What happened to your best friend, Mom?"

"She did just that. She drowned herself in her bathtub because there was no other way out."

I was so young. My mother's words frightened me, although I knew that wasn't her intention.

"Were you part of this pact? Did you have a plan too?"

"Of course; my girlfriends and I all joined in the pact. We each had a different plan to kill ourselves if the Nazis came for us. In the end, it would be better. And that was that, an agreement. It was done."

I couldn't believe my ears. My mother had a suicide pact! Today, I wonder if Mom noticed the look of horror on my face. Probably not, because she was in a world where I didn't belong.

The conversation ended as quickly as it had begun. My mother didn't offer me a comforting hug, nor did I hug my mother. Mom's matter-of-fact attitude was clear. I watched her turn and walk away. I didn't feel like having a sleepover anymore, but Mom's lack of emotion towards this childhood memory made me believe I must be overreacting. I went through with the sleepover, though it didn't bring me the joy such events usually gave me. I have never forgotten Mom's words.

I don't know what triggered my mother that day. It couldn't have been the sleepover — they were a common event in our household. I don't know why Mom told me this particular story, but that was the first and last time I heard Mom discuss something so horrendous from her past.

As I look back, I have three regrets. I wish I had asked my mother the name of her best friend. From time to time, I still think about Mom's friend and her inconceivable desperation. I will never forget her, and it would be nice to know her name.

My second regret is simple. I wish I had thanked my mother for sharing her childhood memory and told her I wanted more.

My third regret is a tough one. I wish I had told Mom I was glad she didn't need to follow through with her girlfriend's pact and hugged her tightly.

Chapter 19

# Not Just a Fox Stole

> These were hard and exciting days.
>
> -VERA OLGA (NAFTHAL) GOLDSTON

**Not one European Jew** would be safe if they remained on the continent. Liza knew the day was coming that the family would need to seek refuge from Nazi persecution; and they would need as much cash as possible to start a new life. Liza also knew the Jews fleeing further into Lithuania would still be in danger. Many wealthy Jews had already left Memel.

Although, Liza had no idea what was left of her marriage, she still wanted Max to leave with her. But there was no question anymore — Vera was leaving with her mother. No matter what, the family came first with the couple — both wife and daughter needed Max.

Liza continued to transfer resources out of the country, but not always in the traditional ways. Max was worried for his wife's safety, but no amount of arguing would discourage her from her mission. Jews were still allowed to move quite freely across the borders, but it was becoming increasingly dangerous. The Nazis, however, didn't want the Jews leaving with large amounts of money or valuables.

Liza was involved in a very risky game. She was clever and an expert with needles and thread. She carefully opened the seams of her lovely fox fur stole — a gift from Max — and then sewed cash and jewellery into the lining. She did the same with the hems of her dresses. Laden with her hidden treasures, Liza traveled back and forth across dangerous borders. Her good looks, fair complexion and ability to speak fluent German did not trigger the border guards' suspicions.

One day, Liza arrived at a German border and presented her papers to the Nazi guards who were busy chatting among themselves. With a nod from the guard, Liza continued through. A woman behind Liza showed her papers and received the same nod to cross. But just as the woman was about to walk away, a piece of silverware fell from her coat sleeve, dropping to the ground with a dreadful clank. As the sound rang out, the world froze. Then a gunshot pierced the air, followed by the thump of the woman's body as she dropped dead to the ground. The Nazi guards resumed their chatter. Liza continued to walk without looking back.

If Liza were caught, she would also be shot dead instantly. What would become of Vera and Max then? But there was nothing else to be done. She continued to smuggle their money and valuables out of Lithuania.

---

I still have memories of my grandmother's fox stole and the seams where it was resewn. What Nanny didn't tell me were the details — when and where. Late in 1938, the borders around Memelland were not controlled by the Nazis. This incident would not have happened crossing a Lithuanian border.

But on October 5, 1938, the passports of German Jews were deemed invalid, and all German Jews were required to surrender their recent passports. To validate the document, the Nazis stamped the passports with the letter 'J' to indicate the holder was a Jew. This made it extremely dangerous for German Jews to travel across their borders.

My theory comes from my research on border crossings in late 1938. Nanny stuffed her fox fur stole with money and valuables; then left her home in Memel and travelled by train through Lithuania. She had to continue through risky regions of Poland arriving in Germany. Once Nanny arrived, Nazis were everywhere and extremely dangerous for any Jews, German or not. My grandmother travelled in and out of Germany to reach her final destination in Paris, France. She faced fierce Nazi guards at every border crossing to successfully reach her French bank account where she secured her money and valuables. Then she returned to Memel to repeat the dangerous trip. Nanny was in great danger in the late months of 1938, however, this was common practice among wealthy Jews. For many years after the war, foreign bank accounts were searched for Jewish fortunes.

---

In 2006, a lawyer contacted my grandmother's second cousin, Alex Cukierman, from the Isserlin side of the family. The lawyer had found a Swiss bank account belonging to Nanny's younger brother, my Great-Uncle Grisha. Uncle Grisha made his money in the same way as his father before him — as a merchant. He and his wife, Aniela, lived in Warsaw, Poland, before WWII. The couple was brutally murdered during the Holocaust. No one would have known about the bank account if it hadn't been for this lawyer. The lawyer worked on a contingency basis, charging thirty percent of the total amount recovered in the Swiss bank account as a finder's fee. This was not an unusual practice and Alex agreed and quickly found and contacted my brother, Jack, with the news.

After our grandparents passed, our family lost touch with my grandmother's cousins living in Israel. My brother exchanged messages back and forth and then opened a bank account, providing Alex with the account number. Soon a deposit was received. The lawyer deducted his thirty percent and the remaining seventy percent was split into three shares. The families in Israel received their two shares, while the Canadian branch of the family tree received the third share. My Goldston/Nafthal family split our share evenly among the five siblings. Several years later, Jack was visiting Israel and had the opportunity to meet Alex for a pleasant lunch.[55]

The money I received was a direct inheritance from my Uncle Grisha, and the significance of that inheritance far outweighed its dollar value. I think about how desperate my uncle must have been, trapped behind borders with the brutal Nazis close at his heels, helpless to protect himself or his loved ones. How terrifying life must have been. Grisha did the only thing he could — he secured his family's money in a Swiss bank account to provide for them after the Holocaust. For me, this meant he still had hope, and I'm glad of that — even though in the end the Swiss bank account sat untouched for decades.

Chapter 20

# The Situation in Memel Worsens

**Since 1926, Lithuania had** a State of Emergency in place, which prohibited citizens from organizing political meetings or demonstrations. This policy kept the Memel Nazis in order.[56]

But on November 1, 1938, German politicians bullied the Lithuanian government into ending the State of Emergency. To celebrate the Nazis gathered in the streets for a rally and torchlight parade. Several days later, the Nazis created the Memel German Security Service, modeled after the SA (the Nazi policing and security unit). The Nazis were soon marching through Memel's streets which terrorized the Jews.[57]

East Prussia, which bordered Lithuania, belonged to Germany. On November 30, 1938, 30,000 Memel Germans crowded the streets to honour the 'Saviour of East Prussia.[58] Paul Von Hindenburg (1847-1934) was a German WWI military commander and former President of Germany. Although he was already dead, the Germans called him their saviour, and Paul von Hindenburg's memory still inspired the German people.[59] Memel's Jewish residents watched helplessly as their friends and neighbours turned their backs on them and joined the Nazi cause.

Windows in synagogues were destroyed. Shouts of, "Throw off the Lithuanian yoke" and "Join the Fuhrër" rang out in the streets. Once again, swastikas appeared on Jewish properties and Germans blocked entrances to their businesses. Some Jewish business owners attempted to quickly liquidate their assets at cheap prices, but the Nazis had plans to take over all Jewish enterprises.[60]

Many Jews watched the horrific developments in fear and decided to leave. In November 1938, 2.5 million Lithuanian Litas (over 8 million Canadian dollars today) were withdrawn from the city's banks. While it may not seem like a great deal of money now, at the time — it was a traumatic hit to the financial institutions. The desperate Jews tried every avenue to emigrate, but for most, it was too late. Many countries already had long waitlists, and many had imposed a visa ban.[61] Liza knew the Jews who migrated to other regions of Lithuania and Europe would never be safe from the Nazis and the madman who led them.

Then a horrifying event occurred in Germany, sending shock waves throughout Europe and the world.

On November 9 and 10, 1938, the Nazis launched a pogrom against the Jews — *Kristallnacht* — the Night of Broken Glass. The name derives from the shards of broken window glass that littered the streets of Jewish buildings, businesses and synagogues. The violent Nazi attack exploded right across Germany and other parts of Europe. Kristallnacht was the most widely reported incident in all the years of the Holocaust. Jewish homes, schools and hospitals were looted. Buildings were demolished by angry crowds with sledgehammers or burned to the ground. For the first time, a massive group of 30,000 men were rounded up and shipped to concentration camps. Violent beatings resulted in hundreds of deaths. Following

Kristallnacht, there were an estimated six hundred and thirty-eight additional deaths by suicide recorded.[62]

The *Times News* of London observed on November 11, 1938.

> *No foreign propagandist bent upon blackening Germany before the world could outdo the tale of burnings and beatings, of blackguardly assaults on defenseless and innocent people, which disgraced that country yesterday.*[63]

Historians believe that Kristallnacht was the prelude to the 'Final Solution' — the Nazi's plan to rid the world of all Jews. In fact, Kristallnacht was the beginning of the mass murder of six million Jews during the Holocaust.[64]

While Max kept well informed about the latest political developments he continued to believe the insanity would be stopped. In contrast, Liza's fears were growing, and she insisted they leave. But Max still refused. By now, their fighting was constant and the beautiful couple were officially separated — and still, neither one moved out of their apartment.

Chapter 21

# The Final Blow

> Then I could no longer go to a regular school, and so my mother started to work - to smuggle money out, to apply for visas, and to push my father to leave. No way was my mother going to stand by and have something similar to the Russian Revolution if not worse happen to her family. As far as she was concerned, we were leaving.
>
> -VERA OLGA (NAFTHAL) GOLDSTON

**The final blow for** Liza began with the ringing of the front doorbell in early November 1938.

Liza was not expecting anyone. A surprise guest often meant someone was in trouble. Perhaps another Jewish family seeking refuge? There were few servants left, so Liza went to the door herself. She unlocked and opened the door, leaving the safety chain in place. There stood the chauffeur, hat in hand. Liza frowned as the driver motioned his head to the right. Vera was standing straight and proud. She had just left for school an hour earlier — something was wrong. Liza quickly unlatched the chain and flung the door wide open.

Liza wanted this to be nothing but childish nonsense. But deep down, she knew the truth. Still, she hoped she was wrong. She folded her arms across her chest and scowled at her thirteen-year-old daughter.

"What is this nonsense about?"

Vera stared back at her mother. Liza knew but had to ask. If nothing else, it gave her a few more seconds to hope this was not happening.

"Mutti, I was sent home! They lied to me, but I know the truth."

Chills went through Liza. She looked at the chauffeur, but he just shrugged his shoulders.

"What did they say?" Liza asked, unfolding her arms.

"They said this button on my blazer doesn't match the others," Vera said, pulling at the button without looking at her mother. "The headmaster said it was disgraceful to come to school like this."

There was silence, but Vera could feel her mother's shock. She met her eyes.

"The headmaster told me to go home. The teacher said to pack all my things because I would not be coming back. She also said she'd informed our driver to wait for me; I was to go home with him." Vera continued to watch her mother.

There it was, straight out of her daughter's mouth — the harsh reality.

It was true, Vera had lost a uniform button a few days earlier. Unable to find a match, Liza had sewn on a button as close to the original as possible. But this was not about a silly button.

Vera held out an envelope. "The headmaster told me to give this to you." She knew this wouldn't help the shock but it needed to be said; "Other students were sent home too, Mutti, not just me." But

Liza wasn't listening as she tore open the envelope and read the note inside.

The words it contained were all too clear. *No Jews allowed*, with no other reason given. Liza knew no amount of money would give her daughter an education in Europe's current political climate.

It was the final blow.

Liza grabbed Vera and held her protectively against her racing heart for reassurance — but it was an empty gesture. Vera was all too aware of the dangers overshadowing their lives.

In some ways, Vera was secretly happy at the thought of no school. There were plenty of Jewish students already banned from their classrooms, and others whose parents had chosen to keep them home. In fact, by the end of November 1938, there were no Jewish girls registered in Memel's schools.[65] Parents attempted to teach their children themselves, but there were too many other problems to worry about. Vera gladly joined in with the activities of the other Jewish girls. Like most European Jews, their parents agreed with Max. The madness would soon be over, and their children would return to school. Vera knew her mother was right — the family needed to get out fast.

The time was up. There would be no more talk. Liza had made her decision — the family was leaving Europe. If Max did not come with them, so be it.

## Chapter 22

# An Ally

> In the meantime, my dad's best friend from England - a Mr. Frank Urmston, an Englishman through and through, a tall, big man blessed with a huge Jewish nose - was accosted in a German restaurant in Berlin and refused entrance. He became my mother's most staunchest ally.
>
> Frank couldn't make things go fast enough. He used all his influence to help us and to assure my father he would find work in the lumber business once he was settled.
>
> -VERA OLGA (NAFTHAL) GOLDSTON

**Mr. Frank Urmston, an** English businessman, was Max's best friend. Frank often travelled for work throughout Europe, particularly to Germany. He was concerned about the Nazi threats and violence, especially to his Jewish friends and acquaintances. In 1938, Frank travelled to Berlin, where he had an experience one night that nearly scared him to death.

By 1938, German Jews were banned from public places such as hotels, restaurants, shops and libraries. This seemed surreal to Frank and impossible to understand. Frank was not Jewish, but he did have one physical trait that Nazis often attributed to Jewish people. Frank was an extremely big man with a huge nose — and it was the nose that got him into trouble. One evening, he went out to dinner at a popular restaurant. But as he stepped inside, a group of Nazi officers dining there jumped up and blocked his entrance.

"No filthy Jews allowed," the Nazis roared as they surrounded him. The chatter of patrons and clatter of dishes came to an abrupt stop. Within seconds, the noise resumed. No one wanted to be involved or witness something they couldn't control, which might result in their arrest or even death as Jewish sympathizers.

Frank stood in shock and fear. He quickly pulled himself together and insisted he was not Jewish. But the Nazis didn't believe him and ordered him to remove his trousers and undergarments to prove that he wasn't circumcised — the Jewish custom is to circumcise male babies shortly after their birth. Frank refused. Instantly, several of the trigger-happy Nazis unbuckled their holsters and placed their hands on their weapons. Before Frank had a moment to think, the others publicly stripped him. With the evidence in front of them, the Nazis acknowledged their mistake, gave an apology of sorts, and invited Frank into the restaurant. Without a word, Frank pulled up his torn trousers and stormed out of the restaurant. The sound of the Nazis' laughter rang in his ears. His hunger for dinner was gone — he returned to his hotel, packed his bags, and took the first train out of Germany. He never returned.

The moment Frank was back home in England, he contacted his Jewish friends and colleagues throughout Europe. Without holding back, he did his utmost to convince all his Jewish allies to leave the continent immediately — including his best friend Max.

Frank was well aware of the stormy relationship between Liza and Max. He knew Liza was preparing to leave Europe with Vera, and that she would go with or without her husband. After his frightening experience with the Nazis, Frank was now Liza's staunchest ally. Frank wanted Max and his family out of Europe as fast as possible. He reassured his best friend there was a need for experienced timbermen in other nations.

Max knew the Nazis had grown too powerful and no one could stop them. Frank succeeded where Liza could not. Max finally agreed it was time to leave the European continent.

Liza was determined to make it happen and so she couldn't get out fast enough. In the late 1930s, Jews were still able to transfer some household goods out of the country. Liza had their furniture, paintings, linens and other valuable household items packed up in wooden crates. Under the Nazis' noses, the crates were transferred onto a ship sailing to France. Liza still didn't know where the family would end up, but she believed having some familiar belongings might bring them comfort in a strange country.

There was still much more to do for a successful exit. The couple applied for permission to leave through the immigration authorities. This permission had a hefty cost of a five-year estimated income tax price tag, paid in advance. To meet this requirement, Max needed some of the money Liza had already smuggled out of the country. Max was furious.

Chapter 23

# Final Preparations to Leave Memelland

**The day finally arrived** in late 1938, Liza and Vera left Memel. The servants had already been dismissed. Liza had provided them with written references and severance packages; this was all she was able to do. The half-empty apartment echoed, a mournful reminder of their former life.

Liza remembered another departure, her fearful flight from Russia with her brother, Grisha, during the Great War. Neither sibling had any experience living alone, and still, the two walked out the door of their childhood home and into the dangerous world. This time, Liza was leaving with her daughter.

While Liza finished the last-minute preparations, she wished she could help Grisha and his wife who lived in Warsaw. She also worried about her sister Mania and her family who was still living in Wilna, Poland — but there was nothing she could do for them right now. Liza, however, still had hope that something could be done soon.

Liza took a final deep breath. With Max and Vera by her side, she walked out the front door of their apartment for the last time. Liza turned away as Max locked the door. They did not know it then, but their memories of life in Memel would also be locked inside them forever, never to be shared.

The couple knew that high-powered Nazis would take over the apartment — and there was nothing they could do to stop them. Liza and Max stared at each other for a moment longer and silently agreed their fight was done. Without another word, they each took one of Vera's hands, turned and walked away. Liza carried her small suitcase, while Max carried Vera's little bag. Mother and daughter travelled light to avoid bringing attention to themselves. There were no goodbyes, no family or good friends to wish them well. Like many other Jews, Liza and Vera simply disappeared from Memel. Max was booked into a hotel where he would stay until he had taken care of the loose ends of his business. Only then would he leave Lithuania.

Their journey began with a 216 km. chauffeured road trip to Kaunas, the capital of Lithuania. This was the only city in the country where Jews were permitted to pick up their exit visas to cross the Lithuanian border. Max and Liza owned a small apartment in the city that would serve as a haven. For the moment the Nazis were only interested in Memel — Lithuania was still safe.[66]

Chapter 24

# Leaving Lithuania

**Max couldn't help but** worry about his family. Liza and Vera were leaving Lithuania for France — a dangerous journey in those times. Sally was fired because he was a Jew and since then he has been travelling from one European country to another. In each country, Sally applied for a visitor visa, then moved on when it expired. He refused to return to Lithuania until the Nazis were stopped. Felix, another brother, was also preparing to leave Memelland with his girlfriend, Lottie. This left Max's brothers, Nathan and Bernard, his sister, Hanna, and their immediate families — all still in Europe. Max also worried about Liza's siblings, Mania and Grisha, and their families. Both Liza and Max's entire extended families were still living in Lithuania, Germany, Poland or other parts of Europe. So many to worry about.

Max's anxiety about Liza and Vera's well-being became overwhelming. He knew his wife would do everything to keep their daughter safe. He also knew his wife was clever. Still, just one wrong move could cost their lives.

Liza was a successful smuggler. If it had not been for the money she had snuck across the border, the family would have had no hope of ever escaping Europe. Liza was also fortunate to have a light complexion and to speak fluent German, so she blended in. But crossing borders with her daughter brought higher risks. Vera could become a great threat.

Vera was her mother's opposite in appearance. She also spoke with a recognizable Memelland accent. Both her appearance and accent could bring the attention of dangerous people, with potentially deadly results. Crossing the borders to reach their destination would take them through regions in Poland and Germany that were far more dangerous than Lithuania. The Nazis were targeting people who looked and had accents like Vera.

But with the exit visas finally secure in her hands, there was nothing else Liza could do but book the train. The choice was either early morning or late-night departure.[67] Liza chose the late train so that Vera could sleep for the greater part of the trip. Besides, they were less visible in the wee hours.

Before leaving for the station, Liza and Max prepared Vera for the dangerous journey. There would be no second chances. Liza took Vera's hands in her own and gave them a gentle shake. Mother and daughter stared at each other. Liza could see the determination in Vera's eyes — such a strong young child! The girl understood it was too dangerous to stay. Better to leave home and everyone they loved.

"Vera, listen to me. You cannot say one word when we arrive at the train station. Not a single word on the whole trip; nothing — understood?"

Vera nodded. She knew the dangers.

"Your accent tells people where we live. That could be dangerous for us. If someone talks to you, do not respond. Keep your eyes down. I'll talk for you."

Vera nodded again, already preparing for her silent journey.

"Do not ask me for anything," said Liza. "I will make sure you get everything you need. Understood?"

Vera nodded again.

"And no long goodbyes at the train station with Vati. A quick hug like we're going away for a few days, that's all."

Liza, Max, and even Vera knew there were Nazi sympathizers everywhere. The best actors had the greatest chance of escaping. If sympathizers discovered their plans, they would report them to the authorities, anticipating a reward for their information.

Max looked at his daughter. "You need to do exactly what Mutti tells you, Veraushka. Mutti will take good care of you, and you'll both make it safely to France. Now we'll give each other our true last goodbyes right here before we go to the train station." Max pulled his daughter in tightly.

Vera had tears in her eyes, but she didn't let them spill over. She wished Vati was coming with them but knew there was no use pleading.

Max turned to his wife. Her fear wasn't visible, but he knew it was there. He worried they'd left their departure too late. But Liza stood tall and confident — they had to make it through.

Liza and Max knew that Vera also understood the dangers. Already in her young life, their daughter had seen and heard of horrors that no child should ever be exposed to. It was time to leave.

Chapter 25

# Saying Goodbye

> Of course I kept my mouth shut; you did what your parents told you in those days. You just knew what would happen if you didn't!
>
> -VERA OLGA (NAFTHAL) GOLDSTON

**Liza and Vera's dangerous** train journey was scheduled for 19:11.[68]

Well aware of the potential consequences of speaking, Vera kept silent at the train station. She was filled with both excitement and fear. There was no time to linger. She was not a thoughtless child; she knew risks lurked around every corner, and that these dangers might not be recognizable until it was too late.

There was nothing left to do but say a quick goodbye to Vati. Vera wanted to cry and cling to her father, giving him final kisses over and over again. Instead, she did what her parents had told her to do — she smiled, hugged and kissed Vati — one, two, three quick little kisses on her father's cheeks — and didn't cling a second longer.

Then Vera watched Mutti lean into Vati and whisper something in his ear. Vati did not speak. Vera's parents looked at each other for a long moment, hugged quickly, and both turned away.

From their stateroom Vera looked out the window, watching her father's back as he slowly walked away. It was a heartbreaking day for Liza, Max and Vera.

---

Mom was only thirteen years old when she left Lithuania, such a young age to understand the potentially fatal consequences. Her simple statement, "you just knew what would happen if you didn't," told me Mom was well aware of the dangers around her. Her world could explode without notice, and there was nothing Mutti or Vati could do to help.

While I worked on this book, more than eighty years after these events, I suffered the raw emotions of my family's experiences. How do I explain to my family and friends that those horrific years before my birth sometimes feel like they happened just last week?

Chapter 26

# Mother and Daughter

**MOTHER AND DAUGHTER SAT** silently in their stateroom. They stared out the window until Vera got sleepy. Once Vera was asleep, Liza tried to focus on her book. Instead, she watched her young daughter and thought about life — something she didn't often allow herself to do.

She was surprised that leaving Max had been so difficult. Their good life in Memel had deteriorated drastically. Their marriage had suffered from so many terrible fights. Just before boarding the train, she'd whispered to Max not to wait too long. Vera needed her father, and she needed her husband. Liza hoped her last words would hurry Max along before it was too late. She wondered if she would ever see him again.

Liza still loved so many of Max's qualities. He was a good father and a good provider. He was a big-shot spender, generous and kind to everyone. His natural charisma and gusto for life lit up rooms wherever he went. For his part, Max still loved showing off his beautiful, smart wife. But most important, both Liza and Max believed in family, and along with Vera the three of them were just that — family. She looked over at their sleeping daughter and wondered for the hundredth time what would become of them.

Life would be normal once they reached Paris since France was not under Nazi influence — at least, not yet. Liza knew that all of Europe was running out of time.

Liza shook her head. This was not the moment to worry about the future. There were plain-clothed Nazis and Nazi sympathizers everywhere. They could trust no one, nor show any signs of fear. There was no room in Liza's thoughts for failure, only survival.

The train travelled all night through Lithuania, heading towards the Polish border and other dangerous regions for Jews. That winter of 1939, Germany demanded the return of the Polish Corridor, having lost the valuable region to the Polish government after WWI. It was Poland's only connection to the Baltic Sea, but it was also important to the Nazis because it linked East Prussia to Germany. Although the Polish government gave Germany free transit across the Corridor, Hitler wanted more.[69]

The night train carried Liza and Vera straight into the unsettled region of the Polish Corridor. With the doors on the train all securely locked and Polish soldiers standing guard at each access, Liza was still worried.[70] Nazis everywhere were planning their next moves. Liza hoped attacking the train that night was not part of their plans.

An eerie silence filled the train. Liza sat vigil, ready to react at a moment's notice. In the end, the train crossed the Polish Corridor without incident. Once across the border into Germany, the Polish soldiers quickly disappeared.[71] Liza felt alone and vulnerable, but she pulled herself together and shook off her feelings.

The first stop was Berlin, Germany, where they planned to catch their connector train to France. Liza knew the beautiful city well, but now it was extremely dangerous for Jews. She just wanted to safely board the train to France.

As they walked through the Berlin train station, Liza longed to hold Vera close to protect her. But such unusual behaviour with a thirteen-year-old would only bring attention to them. Instead, Liza casually took Vera's hand and they smiled at each other — they looked like mother and daughter travelling together without a care in the world. The confident pair walked through the station to their connecting train, right under the noses of German police and Nazis.

Finally, they arrived in Paris — safe at last. No one could imagine their emotions as Liza and Vera let the porter help them down the steps and out into the station. Mother and daughter looked at each other, smiled and hugged. Liza was very proud of Vera. She'd demonstrated the talents of a skillful actress. They hurried out of the train station and onto the busy streets of Paris. Such relief!

Liza quickly sent a telegram to Max; "All is well."

Max read the message and let out his breath. If Liza and Vera had disappeared he would have been completely devastated. Once again, Max appreciated Liza's strength and determination. Now she had saved their daughter's life.

Chapter 27

# Life in France

> My mother went to visit with her family in Paris. She had only a temporary visa but stayed on none the less, taking a chance on not getting caught. Mutti could not have kept me with her, because I would have had to be registered in school, and so a visa would have had to be produced for both of us.
>
> -VERA OLGA (NAFTHAL) GOLDSTON

LIZA AND MAX HAD applied for refugee status in Australia, Canada and the United States. Liza didn't care which country accepted them, but she was anxious to receive a confirmation soon. In those terrible days, with immigration almost impossible for European Jews, there was absolutely no other plan to consider.

While they waited, Liza and Vera settled into a rooming house in the centre of the city. Unlike Memel, Paris was not yet troubled by the horrors of Nazi politics, which meant that mother and daughter had finally found some relief. They kept a low profile, living quietly. For now, Liza and Vera felt safe enough to enjoy the charms of Paris. But this was short-lived.

Liza's exit visa was about to expire — and this meant trouble. There was a friendly concierge in her building who knew of her predicament. Liza hoped she could trust him, and her good fortune prevailed. The concierge didn't ask questions about her visa or speak of her situation to anyone.

Because Liza's visa was about expire, Vera couldn't be registered for school. And, Liza would soon be an illegal immigrate. As an illegal immigrant, Liza could be deported back to Memelland and into the hands of the Nazis. If the French authorities were to deport Liza, Vera would also be sent back with her mother.

But Liza was clever. Foreseeing this situation, she had applied for a British student visa for Vera, which was approved. In the event of trouble spreading to England, Liza did not want Vera to attend a Jewish boarding school. Her stubborn daughter insisted despite her mother's wishes, and Liza finally gave in to Vera's demands. At least Liza knew that Vera would be treated well by other Jewish students and staff. In early 1939, Liza and Vera travelled to the safety of a Jewish boarding school outside of London.

Both mother and daughter were disappointed they couldn't stay together. After all they had been through, Liza worried about leaving Vera but there was nothing else to be done. Once Vera was settled in school, Liza returned to Paris, taking her chances as an illegal immigrant.

Chapter 28

# An English Boarding School

> I finally got a student visa for England and insisted on a Jewish school - which I hated once I was there, but at least I was safe.
>
> What went on in the private synagogue I was too young and too ignorant to appreciate at the time. After all I was an only child, no brothers and most of my friends had no brothers either. I realized what went on and what I was playing guard to. My parents would have had a fit had they known what education I was getting for all their money.
>
> -VERA OLGA (NAFTHAL) GOLDSTON

A JEWISH BOARDING SCHOOL was just what Vera wanted — but it didn't take long before she discovered her big mistake.

The priority in choosing a boarding school was that they teach English. Both Liza and Vera knew that wherever they emigrated, English would be their first language. Vera was good at languages and looked forward to these classes, but to her great disappointment, she soon learned the school did not teach the mandatory English. Most of the students were from Germany, and only German was spoken.

Vera also had complaints about the food. She was accustomed to a personal cook, pampering her with favourite dishes. As a result of her father's passion for five-star cuisine, Vera had developed a good palate. She was used to dining in the finest restaurants with the most popular chefs. The kitchen in her boarding school produced dreadful meals. Six mornings a week she began the day hungry, giving away her bland breakfast; but on the seventh day, many students gave her a wonderful treat — a plateful of kippers. On these mornings most students began the day with hunger pains, while Vera plowed her way through a heap of tasty smoked herring.

Both boys and girls attended the school, with Vera among the youngest of the pupils. The older children often asked the younger ones to play 'watch guard' with them in the synagogue. Playing with boys was never part of Vera's life. In Memel, she only had girlfriends. As a watch guard, Vera had no idea what the older boys and girls were doing in the shadows of the temple until she peeked. She knew Mutti and Vati would never approve. Her parents would have had a fit if they knew what education she was receiving for their money.

What was most important for the time being was that Vera was settled and safe.

---

Decades later, Mom laughed when she thought back to what she learned at boarding school playing this silly game. "Heaven forbid that Mutti should ever open her mouth to tell me about such things as sex. Never!" claimed my mother.

Chapter 29

# Liza in Paris

> I was safe in England, and that was the main thing at the time.
>
> —VERA OLGA (NAFTHAL) GOLDSTON

**Liza woke up worried** about her daughter every morning. She believed England would eventually be invaded by the Nazis, but hoped not before she first got Vera out safely. If there was trouble, Liza had no legal visa to cross the border to fetch her child, nor would the borders be safe. But no matter what happened, if needed, she was determined to find a way.

Liza's thoughts went to her husband as well. The Nazi's presence was increasing in Memel, and yet Max was still determined to stay. If Liza was deported, what would become of her daughter and husband?

Liza needed to keep her sanity while she waited, and so she decided to spend her time preparing herself for her new life. Liza could manage a household, but she knew nothing about cooking and domestic work. She had no idea what skills she would need, but cooking seemed like a good place to start.

The finest culinary school in Paris was the world-renowned Le Cordon Bleu. For her first class, Liza prepared the perfect poached egg on toast. She had no idea how important her cooking skills would become in the future.

---

My grandmother and I both attended world-renowned culinary schools in our mid-years. Liza attended the famous Le Cordon Bleu in Paris. Years later, famous American chef Julia Child enrolled in the same institute. My grandmother loved watching Julia Child on television.

I attended a culinary school in eastern Canada and enrolled in the famous Culinary Institute of America in Hyde Park, New York. I attended classes in Cakes, Tarts, Torts and Contemporary Pastries. Although we both received professional training, neither Nanny nor I ever worked as chefs in professional kitchens in the culinary arts industry.

Chapter 30

# Max Prepares to Leave

> Vati stayed in Memel looking after his business interests as long as he could. He was still reluctant to leave; in spite of all the rumors, he felt that Hitler would be stopped and would not take Memelland.
>
> -VERA OLGA (NAFTHAL) GOLDSTON

MAX SPENT MOST OF his time focused on his business, but his thoughts also frequently turned to his wife. He knew that Liza had made a good home for him, and he missed that. He received regular telegrams from his wife urging him to leave Lithuania, and his friends were strongly suggesting the same.

Even with the difficulties in Memel, he held onto hope that the craziness would come to an end. Max was a fair and generous man, which meant he had many loyal friends and servants. Perhaps he believed he was well protected from the Nazis; after all, who would want to hurt him? Little did Max know, that loyalties meant nothing in these troubled times.

Max spent his days close to his work and the hotel where he lived. His business was doing surprisingly well. Many Jews were attempting to sell their businesses cheaply, but Max refused to sell for a low price, and instead gave his brother Nathan power of attorney over his properties. This was a good business decision. Nathan was able to keep Max's properties and business safe under his Lithuanian passport, which provided some protection from the German Reich at that time.

By now, there were many reasons why it was too late for Nathan to leave the country. The Nazis often watched him, never seeming to tire of this surveillance, and they made it impossible for him to obtain an exit visa. Besides, his wife, Helene, was suffering from cancer. She would never pass the medical examination required for immigration, and Nathan would not leave his wife behind. Instead, Nathan and his family would have to endure the political turmoil. As Max prepared his brother to assume all responsibility for his assets, neither of them imagined the horrific consequences that would result from Nathan staying in Lithuania.

Max's extended family, and his Isserlin in-laws would be staying in Europe, except for brothers Sally and — Felix and his girlfriend Lottie. Max could not imagine being separated from his family, however, the reality that Memel would soon be annexed by German was becoming clearer.

## Chapter 31

# A Close Call

> Vati kept going as usual - until one day a friend warned him the Nazis were moving the borders and he had better get out. His chauffeur kept delaying departure, and my father, guessing he was a Nazi, kicked him out of the car and then took off himself, driving full speed ahead to the border.
>
> -VERA OLGA (NAFTHAL) GOLDSON

**While Max was still** living in Memel, a good friend with Nazi connections informed him that Hitler's troops were preparing to cross the border and invade Memel. The loyal friend advised Max to get out of the country while he still could. He also told Max that his chauffeur was a Nazi sympathizer, whose orders were to detain Max at any cost. Max was appalled to learn of his employee's betrayal. He had always trusted his chauffeur and had always been generous to him and his family.

On March 22, 1939, the Nazis annexed Memel into the German Reich. On that same day, just hours before the invasion, Max's brother Nathan fled Memel with his wife, Helene, and their children Ursula (Ulla) and Alfred (Alf). The family went to Kaunas, the same city from which Liza and Vera had caught the train to France only a few months earlier. The Nazis had no interest in Kaunas for the time being, and so it remained untouched. Nathan moved his family into Max and Liza's four-room furnished flat, and life seemed more normal in the capital city. Nathan continued to run his lumber company and took complete control over Max's business as well. The family hoped to stay in Kaunas until the trouble was over. Tragically, this is not how the events played out.

On March 23, 1939, one day after the annexation, Adolf Hitler arrived in Memel Harbour on board a German battleship. SS officers (Schutzstaffel, or Protection Squads), police units and Hitler Youth groups assembled alongside German citizens in the crowded streets, all wanting to see and hear Hitler. Swastika flags were everywhere.[72] Hitler used his bullhorn to broadcast his speech through the city, though Max was not in the crowd, he could still hear the German Führer. The rage and hatred in Hitler's voice made Max shudder with fear.

By order of the Nazi regime, the remaining Jews in Memel were required to leave the city within fourteen days or be arrested. To make matters worse, Memel Harbour was now closed to the Jews, making it impossible for them to flee the city by way of the Baltic Sea.[73]

The Nazis were stunned to see how the Jews in Memel were still operating their businesses openly and freely. Since the night of Kristallnacht in Germany, the Nazis believed Memel's Jews would have fled, leaving their businesses behind. They were also surprised that the established Party in Memel hadn't already confiscated Jewish goods and properties.[74]

On March 24, 1939, the local Memel paper *Volkischer Beobachter,* which was now under Nazi control, published the following article.

> *In the early morning already, two trains overfilled with Jews departed Memel once more; yesterday evening a train likewise left Memel that was so overfilled with Jews that some of the passengers stood on the running boards. The population of Memel gave these Jewish freeloaders, under whose influence it has suffered for decades, their farewell. Upon news of the large flight of the Jews, thousands of people appeared at the train station, and the numerous taxis that arrived, packed with household goods, bedding, etc. were greeted with all kinds of hilarious acclamations. Groups of chanters formed on the railway platform, calling to the Jews: "We wish you a good trip and never-see-you-again!" or "Travel to Abraham!"*

Max's last chance to flee his homeland came quickly, with no plan or preparation. But first, he had to deal with his chauffeur. If Max confronted him or fired him: the consequences would be fatal. Instead, Max summoned his chauffeur and ordered him to drive to the Memel/Lithuania border. But the chauffeur kept delaying their departure, until finally, at Max's insistence, they started for the border with Max sitting on the right side of the back seat.

The chauffeur took a different route than usual. "A shortcut, Herr Nafthal, that is all."

Max had never imagined himself in such a predicament, on the edge of falling into the hands of the dreaded Nazis. He felt his fear gather in the form of sweat at the nape of his neck, instantly soaking the back of his pristine dress shirt. He couldn't stop the slight tremor in his damp hands. But there was no time — he had to do something. He took a deep breath, and the instinct to survive shot through his whole being, cleared his head, and gave him the strength to act.

"*Ja,* this is good, a shortcut," Max said, surprising himself at how calm he sounded.

"*Ja,* this is good," agreed the chauffeur, taking his eyes off the road for just a second to glance back and smile at Max.

"But I can't leave without a supply of my favorite cigars," said Max. "Pull over at that tobacco shop so I can stock up."

The chauffeur took his eyes off the road for a second time and looked at his boss. Then he nodded.

Once the automobile came to a stop, Max handed the chauffeur some money. He also told him to buy a pack of cigarettes for himself.

As Max had anticipated, the chauffeur was thrilled at the offer of free cigarettes. "*Ich danke Ihnen.*" He turned the car off, grabbed the keys from the ignition and opened the door.

"*Nein*, leave the keys."

The chauffeur looked back at Max in shock.

"I'm chilled. Perhaps it's my nerves," said Max.

The chauffeur stared hard at Max. Then he smiled, tossed the keys in the air, caught them, inserted the key back in the ignition, and started the car to turn on the heat.

Max waited until the chauffeur was inside the shop, then quickly got out of the back seat and ran around the car to get into the driver's seat. He wiped his sweaty hands on his coat and gripped the steering wheel. Then he shifted gears, jerked the car into drive, floored the gas peddle, and sped away with squealing tires straight for the Memelland border.

Before the annexation of Memel, the Nazis had no authority at the Memelland border. But that changed on March 22, 1939.[75] When Max arrived at the border and rolled down his window to talk with the guards, he was shocked to learn that the border was closed to all

Jews. His exit visa meant nothing. The border guards showed Max the Nazis 'Most Wanted' list, and his name was at the top. Unable to drive further, Max sat in his car, mere feet away from safety.

Max, however, had used this border crossing often, and the guards knew him well. Over the years, they had benefitted from his generosity. Max knew the men were poorly paid, and so he often helped them with money and clothing for their families. Now to repay him, the grateful guards raised the barrier and waved him through. Max's previous acts of compassion had saved his life.

Max continued to the capital city, Kaunas where he continued to work and apply for visitor visas from neighbouring countries. He hired another chauffeur who came highly recommended by trust-worthy friends. Then days later, and for unknown reasons, Max returned to the border to re-enter Memelland. The same guards were on duty, but this time they informed Max it was too dangerous to let him pass.

The guards told Max that the Nazis had arrived only thirty minutes after he'd crossed to safety several days earlier. They had a warrant for Max's arrest. "Have you seen the Jew Nafthal?" they'd demanded.

Max's crime? Born a Jew, punishable with imprisonment, hard labour, starvation and brutal murder. Perhaps, the Nazis would use a bullet to the head, leave Max's body where it dropped and drive away in his vehicle. In any case, the border guards turned Max away that day, saving his life for a second time.

There was nothing for Max to do but turn back. He received papers to visit Latvia soon after, and so he traveled by land to the city of Libau, hoping another visa would be approved before the Latvian visa expired. Neighbouring countries did not allow Jews to immigrate, though Jews still moved across one border to the next using visitor visas with expiry dates of only a week or two.

Lithuania and Poland's borders were closed for many years, making it almost impossible to travel freely back and forth. But in 1938, they agreed to open their borders, hoping to grow stronger together in the face of the extreme pressure posed by Nazi threats. This was a stroke of good luck for Max. With his Latvian visitor visa about to expire, Max and his new chauffeur made their way to Gdansk Port in Danzig, Poland. Although the Nazis did not annex Poland until September 1, 1939, Danzig's population was ninety percent German. Many plainclothes Nazis and Nazi sympathizers were working underground, watching, listening and informing on Jews and Jewish activity in the area. This was not a safe place for Max, but his choices were limited.

Once Max arrived at Gdansk Port, he quickly boarded a boat for Nynashamn, Sweden. While his ship was leaving the harbour, Max looked back through binoculars. His heart was in his throat as he watched Nazis arrive in large, black vehicles to surround his empty car with their guns drawn. It was a third close call; he could not afford another.

Max's Swedish visitor visa was only a few days from expiring when he received another. He set off again, this time departing from Grebbestad, Sweden, and arriving in Skagen, Denmark. When his Danish visa was about to expire, Max hired a car and made his way to Holland, where he stayed with friends for a few weeks. Just before that visitor visa expired, he travelled by land to Belgium and then back to his friends in Holland.

Max was extremely fortunate. Though his visas were only valid for a week or two, they were often difficult to obtain. If Max's visa had expired in any of these countries, he would have been sent back to Lithuania and into the hands of the dreaded Nazis.

One day while Max was in Holland, he finally received good news from Liza that Canada had approved the family's immigration application. With this, Liza immediately received a new visitor's visa from France. The Canadian immigration application included Liza, Max and Vera, as well as Max's two brothers Sally, Felix and Lottie, whom Felix had recently married. Sally had fled Lithuania before Max and was travelling around Europe applying for one visitor visa after another. And Felix and Lottie were likely doing the same.

Within days of receiving this news, the family was also accepted by the United States and Australia. But the red tape involved in American immigration was extremely complicated, and Australia was too far away from their homeland. Therefore, it was decided that the Nafthal family would wait out Europe's political chaos in Canada.

Canadian immigration requirements for European Jews came with strict conditions as well as a large price tag — only much-needed labourers or the wealthy were accepted. In the late 1930s, the Canadian economy desperately needed strong farm labourers or people wealthy enough to purchase operating farms. This became a requirement for European Jews applying for Canadian immigration, and consequently, most applications were rejected.

Max's brother Felix was thrilled. He could easily transfer his skills as a professional racehorse trainer to farming. Max, on the other hand, knew nothing about land or agriculture — but he did have a successful track record in business, and wealth enough to purchase a working farm. Liza had checked the 'farmer' box on their immigration application, which came with a seven-year commitment.

Each approved immigrant was assigned to a province and region according to that province's needs. The Nafthal family's destination was rural Nova Scotia, in eastern Canada. The small province had an abundance of good fertile land and was desperate for farmers. Liza and Max had never heard of Nova Scotia — nor did they know anything about rural living — but that didn't matter in the circumstances.

The Nafthal family accepted all the required conditions of their immigration. It was an interesting merging of cultures, not only for the wealthy European city dwellers but for Nova Scotia's rural residents as well. Most locals had never met a European before — let alone a Jewish family.

Chapter 32

# The Medicals

> Vati had a bit of a trouble, as he always had a very bad rash on one leg and the doctor would not pass him. He went to a specialist who told him, that as he probably already knew, there was nothing to be done about the rash.
>
> -VERA OLGA (NAFTHAL) GOLDSTON

**With Liza's Canadian immigration** approved and her French visitor visa in hand, it was finally safe for Vera to be reunited with her mother. Liza went to England and brought her daughter back to Paris.

The immigration paperwork was almost complete, and proof of good health was the final requirement for refugee status. This entailed a simple medical examination by an approved Canadian immigration physician. Liza and Vera breezed through their preliminary medical tests — but Max was another story.

Over the years, Max had seen doctors about a persistent rash on his leg. The doctors had informed him nothing could be done, and so Max failed his preliminary medical examination. His refugee status would not be accepted while he had this skin irritation. Max was still in Holland. He went to a Dutch specialist who confirmed what Max already knew — there was no cure for the rash. The specialist recognized his patient's predicament and its consequences. If Max was sent back to Memel, a Nazi death sentence waited for him. Wanting to help, the specialist offered a temporary cure so that Max could pass the second medical.

Thanks to the specialist's kindness, Max received a clean bill of health for his Canadian refugee status. He also obtained a French visitor visa, allowing him to finally reunite with his wife and daughter in Paris.

After six months apart, Liza, Max and Vera were together again. They had several weeks to spare before boarding their ship for Canada. The family celebrated with a holiday, enjoying the sights and relishing the famous French cuisine. Feeling safe in France, Max started to complain again about leaving Europe. Liza had to put up with his grumbling for some time.

In late June 1939, the family left France and traveled by ship to London, England. Liza wanted Vera to meet her father's old friend, the vice-president of His Master's Voice, the man Liza's father, Mark Isserlin, had met on the train so many years ago. This was the same man who had offered her father the contract for the first phonograph sales for all of Russia or the United States. Liza's thought about her parents and childhood in Russia which wasn't something she often allow herself to do.

Max reunited with his brother Sally, who would travel with them to Canada. Felix and Lottie had tickets to travel separately on May 29, 1939, aboard the *Duchess of Bedford*, leaving from Liverpool, England.

On June 30, Max and his family boarded the *Duchess of York* and set sail for Canada. Liza, Max, Vera and Sally had made it safely onto the ship. Their departure was just two months before the beginning of World War II.

Liza and Max believed they'd return to Memel one day after the brutal chaos and madness were over. For now, Vera believed she was on the greatest adventure of her life.

---

Decades later, Mom claimed she remembered the visit to His Master's Voice vividly. She wrote she had always intended to find the family friend and reconnect with him, but she never did. The old gentleman must have made a huge impression on my mother, but despite my attempts to find his name and family, his identity remains unknown.

---

I was surprised to discover the family left England from Liverpool Harbour, as I had my own 'connection' with the city. By 1964, the Beatles were making an international sensation with Beatlemania — and the members of the rock band were from Liverpool, England. As a thirteen-year-old, I loved the Beatles and all the mania that surrounded them. I had posters and pictures of the rock stars plastered all over my bedroom. Imagine my shock decades later after my mother's death, when I discovered she had left her homeland from Liverpool and never told me. I wonder if Mom thought back to her departure in,1939, during my Beatlemania craze. I wish Mom had talked to me.

Chapter 33

# The Duchess of York

> We finally took off on the Duchess of York from Liverpool and landed for immigration in Quebec, then on to Montreal. Mutti had some introductions to people there. We looked around, at what after London and Paris appeared to us a very small city.
>
> -VERA OLGA (NAFTHAL) GOLDSTON

**As the ship slowly** pulled away from the Liverpool pier, the family stood on deck waving to a small crowd of strangers back onshore. No family members nor friends were there to bid them farewell. As land disappeared, the family made themselves familiar with the ship. That's when the reality of what they were doing hit Max.

Max entered a state of high anxiety, worrying about the fate of his timber business back home and the family's future in a foreign land. His uncertainties were legitimate because he did not speak English and knew nothing about farming. Liza assured Max that everything would work out, but Max thought it was foolishness and still wanted to go home. Fortunately, Vera seemed quite content with the changes.

One afternoon, Vera was curled up on a deck chair with her feet tucked under her writing postcards to her girlfriends. "So far, so good," Liza thought to herself.

After completing her postcards, Vera handed them to the porter to post in the mail. Liza happened to glance down and read one of her daughter's cards. Vera had written three words to her best friend; "*Open to Consummation.*" It was fourteen-year-old Vera's way of sharing that since leaving Memel, she had started her menstrual cycles.[76] A bit of a prude on such topics, Liza was mortified at her daughter's carefree comment written on the back of a postcard for anyone to read. Luckily for Vera Mutti got over such things quickly. Given the fierce political situation in Memel, Vera's girlfriend likely never received her postcard. In any event, there was no response.

As they sailed farther away from their home, Liza, Max, and Sally grieved for everything they were leaving behind — their family, their friends, and their community with its traditions, both religious and not. They ached for the vibrant city of Memel and the elaborate lifestyle it had offered. They remembered all the people who had taken care of them — the cooks, housemaids, seamstresses and chauffeurs always at their beck and call. What would become of them now?

Reality sank in. They were Jewish refugees seeking political asylum, on a ship carrying them closer to rural Nova Scotia. If that wasn't enough, Liza and Max had agreed to become farmers — and they had no idea what owning and operating a farm would entail. Nor could they visualize life in rural Nova Scotia. And truth be known, rural Nova Scotia couldn't picture them either!

Just before the ship made its first stop in Canada, two Germans jumped overboard. The two were presumed to be Nazi spies who were picked up by a French-Canadian boat. They were never heard of again.

The *Duchess of York* made its first stop in Quebec City. The Nafthals were required to register with Canadian Immigration to receive final refugee status. Liza, Max, Vera and Sally disembarked, walked into the terminal, and stood before the immigration officer. The Nafthals and the officer stared at one another, neither side knowing what the other was thinking. Liza understood English and answered the routine questions. While the family looked on, the border guard stamped each passport in turn. With a smile at Liza, the guard handed back the passports. "Welcome to Canada!"

Vera knew enough English to understand what had just happened, but Max and Sally wanted confirmation. When Liza smiled, the men's faces filled with relief. "Welcome to Canada! We're safe!" Liza cried out. No one had ever seen such happy faces! That moment marked the beginning of a lifetime of gratitude to Canada and its people.

Canada's newest Jewish European immigrants reboarded the *Duchess of York* to sail on to Montreal. They were finally free from Nazi Germany — or so they thought.

---

On May 13, 1939, the MS *St. Louis* set sail from Hamburg, Germany, for Cuba, just one month before Liza and Max boarded the *Duchess of York*. *St. Louis* was a German luxury ocean liner. It carried 937 passengers, most of whom were German Jewish refugees escaping Nazi persecution. Their paperwork was in order, and all passengers had been accepted by Cuban Immigration.

But on May 27, *St. Louis* was prevented from docking at Havana Harbour in Cuba. All permits and visas issued before May 5 were revoked, leaving only 29 passengers with permission to disembark. One passenger had died on the voyage — which meant that 907 passengers were now stranded on the ocean liner.

On June 2, *St. Louis* left Cuba and set sail for Florida. Like the Cubans, American officials denied the frantic refugees asylum. Captain Gustav Schroder was desperate but refused to give up. The ship was only two days away from Halifax, Nova Scotia, and that's where the ship headed next. Although frantic attempts were made to aid the Jewish passengers, Canada also refused them asylum.

Halifax Harbour was my family's final destination. They would have heard about the *St. Louis'* troubles. With no alternative, *St. Louis* returned to Europe. In the end, the United Kingdom, France, Belgium and the Netherlands agreed to split the passengers and grant asylum to the Jewish refugees.

With this story in their thoughts, my family had much to worry about during their voyage to Nova Scotia. They would not have rested well until they had successfully passed through Immigration and stood on Canadian soil for the first time.

In May 1940, the German Nazis invaded France, Belgium and the Netherlands — three of the four countries that took in the *St. Louis'* passengers.[77]

In January 2011, a memorial sculpture was unveiled at the Canadian Museum of Immigration at Pier 21 in Halifax Harbour — the same pier where *St. Louis* would have docked. The *Wheel of Conscience* honours the ship's refugees. The impressive stainless-steel monument includes four gears; the first gear, named *hatred,* turns into increasingly larger gears of *racism, xenophobia* and *anti-*

*Semitism*. The names of all the passengers are also listed on the monument.[78]

---

In 1939, when asked how many Jews should be accepted into the country, a high-level Canadian official from William Lyon Mackenzie King's government responded — *None is too many.* Leading up to and during WWII, King's government had many anti-Semitic members and supportive citizens who alleged a large amount of European Jewish refugees threatened Canadian society; believing Jews would not adapt to the laws of Canada, nor would they change their cultural and religious beliefs to fit into Canada's society. From 1933 to 1945, according to Irving Abella and Harold Troper, authors of *None is Too Many* claimed Canada admitted less than 5,000 European Jewish refugees while the USA admitted more than 200,000, Palestine 125,000 and Britain 70,000. Canada ranked the lowest number of refugees among the developed nations. My grandparents must have been aware of Canada's anti-Semitic government. [79]

On November 7, 2018, Canada's Prime Minister Justin Trudeau delivered a formal apology in the House of Commons for Canada's role in the fate of the ship, *St. Louis* and its passengers. Trudeau apologized to the passengers, their families, and Jewish communities in Canada and around the world.[80]

---

In 2019, a survey by the Azrieli Foundation of Toronto found that the majority of Canadians lack knowledge of the Holocaust. Sixty-two percent of millennials did not know that six million Jews were brutally murdered during the Holocaust. More disturbing, twenty-two percent of millennials had never even heard of the Holocaust. Fifty-two percent of younger Canadians and forty-nine percent of Canadians overall could not name one of the more than 40,000 concentration camps, ghettos, and other incarceration sites. Thirty-two percent of survey respondents also believed Canada had an open immigration policy for Jews fleeing persecution in Europe.[81]

Naomi Azrieli, CEO and Chair of the Azrieli Foundation, stated that she was "shocked and disappointed to see the Canadian results. There are holes in our education system that must be filled because as it stands now, we are not preparing the next generation to learn from the past."[82]

---

My grandparents and mother were grateful to their adopted country. I never heard them say a negative word about Canada; they loved this country and were happy here. As a child, my family taught me to love and respect our country as well. I cannot believe so much awareness has been lost concerning WWII and the Holocaust. I hope our young people will take an interest and learn about this horrendous period of history — and then share what they've learned with others to ensure it never happens again.

---

Shawnigan Lake School on Vancouver Island, BC, is one school that hosts an annual Holocaust & Genocide Symposium for its student body, staff and guests. For the past number of years, I've been invited to this event. The school is an easy drive from my home, and when I'm not travelling, I always attend. It is greatly appreciated.

Chapter 34

# A Brief Stay in Montreal

> I was offered a hot dog but refused, as I was not used to eating dog meat.
>
> -VERA OLGA (NAFTHAL) GOLDSTON

**The family collected their** luggage from the ship and left the port to visit the city of Montreal. Vera was bursting with excitement and she loved every single moment of their new adventure.

When they reached the hotel on Sainte-Catherine Street, Liza took a deep breath. They had made it — their life in Canada was about to start. Soon they would see what could be done for the others left in Europe, but for now, this was Liza's moment.

Montreal was a small town compared to London or Paris. But who cared? What mattered was that the desk clerk addressed them as "Mister and Madame," not "Jew and Jewess Nafthal." What a relief!

They weren't going to be alone, because Liza brought several Montreal introductions from European connections. Most residents in Montreal were bilingual in French and English, and Vera was looking forward to chatting away in French with whoever would listen. People did need to pay attention when they communicated with Vera in the

Montreal dialect and western terminology — because she was easily confused.

With Mutti's contacts, the family was soon swept up in social events. Everyone wanted to welcome the new immigrants and receive firsthand news from Europe.

Vera received an invitation to a young girl's birthday party — her first Canadian social event without her parents. She wondered if the birthday celebration would be different from parties at home. Vera knew Mutti was an expert shopper so they had no trouble finding the perfect gift and a pretty dress for Vera to wear.

Despite their preparations, Mutti and Vati were nervous as they dropped Vera off. At fourteen years old, Vera felt grown-up — so why did her parents look so worried? What could go wrong? Vera wasn't a shy girl. She could get by with a little English and struggle through the strange French lingo — almost.

The birthday gift was a huge success and all the girls loved Vera's new dress. Such things are so important to a teenager, especially when you're the new girl. Vera loved the loud western music — A-*Tisket, A-Tasket* by Ella Fitzgerald and Chick Webb, and *Shortenin' Bread* by the Andrew Sisters. By now, Vera could even pick out a few words from the songs. She had great fun learning the latest dance moves to *Boomps-A-Daisy,* lifting her dress a little on one side as she swung her hips to touch another guest — just like the girls taught her. Vera was not blessed with rhythm, so she danced completely offbeat and knew it. But Vera was always a confident girl, and she was having the time of her life with her new friends.

It was great fun attending a birthday party where none of the girls discussed Adolf Hitler or Nazi Germany. Nor did they talk about violent Gestapo round-ups and frightening suicide pacts. The

Canadian girls knew nothing of Vera's past horrors, and she would never tell them. Why would she break this wonderful spell?

"Finally," thought Vera. "Everything in my life is as it should be."

Then *it* happened!

The hostess offered the girls a hotdog-in-a-bun. Vera's smile disappeared as she watched the other girls gather at the dining room table. She not only refused the hotdog, she quickly retreated to the corner of the dining room, as far away from the table as possible. When asked what was wrong, she insisted her parents be called to fetch her. After several failed attempts to make sense of her distress, Vera's parents were called.

"No, we don't know what happened," the hostess told Liza in English over the phone. Vera was too upset to understand any of the one-sided discussion.

She waited for her parents at the large picture window in the living room. She was ready to bolt the moment she saw the car come around the corner but mindful of her manners, she waited for Mutti and Vati.

"What happened?" Mutti asked the moment she saw Vera.

"They eat dog meat," Vera informed her parents in German, so no one else would understand. "They offered me dog meat in-a-bun!"

Mutti's right eyebrow rose ever so slightly. Vati's eyes widened, and his whole face reddened. Father and daughter stared at Mutti. They waited for her to fix the problem. The hosts and girls stood a few meters away, anxiously waiting for an explanation.

Mutti looked at Vera, then at the hosts. They did not teach one how to address such situations in finishing school. "Please do not be offended. I am sorry, but we are not accustomed to eating dog meat. I do hope you understand?"

The hosts were so stunned, that they first thought they'd misunderstood Liza's strong Russian accent. Then suddenly it all made sense, and laughter rang out. The hostess explained the misunderstanding to Liza, who in turn explained it to her husband and daughter. Everyone laughed together. And Vera's response to her mother? "Why couldn't they just call it a wiener and make me happy?"

Chapter 35

# Halifax, Nova Scotia

> But lots of things were strange; we missed the rye bread and rolls you bought in Europe at every street corner. Pies and cakes tasted weird at first. I missed the many kinds of fish and salamis and raw ham. To compensate, I gorged myself on bananas, which had been a rarity in my life; I adored milkshakes and loved ice cream. But what did food matter? There was so much to be learned and to be seen, a great big wonderful world in front of us, such as we had never encountered. I had a glorious time. But my parents were not so happy.
>
> -VERA OLGA (NAFTHAL) GOLDSTON

**In 1937, Halifax was** a small, gritty city suffering through the Great Depression. City officials were shocked at an unwelcome interest from overseas — the German airship *Hindenburg* astonished Halifax residents as it hovered above their city. The Germans took photographs of the harbour, the dockyards, and Citadel Hill, a fortress overlooking the harbour. Adolf Hitler was secretly developing a plan for worldwide domination, and even the small seaport of Halifax played a part in these plans.[83]

Germany was interested in Halifax's harbour, which had been used during the First World War. There were many advantages from a military point of view. Halifax's natural harbour was large and deep, which meant that in winter the waters were ice-free. As well, the port was close to the Great Circle shipping route from Europe to the Eastern Seaboard of North America. The Halifax immigration facility on Pier 21 was designed to take in ocean liners, which meant it could also accommodate large troopships and other vessels. If war did break out, the ocean terminals could easily support both civilian and military traffic.[84]

---

In mid-June, 1939, Liza and Max prepared to leave Montreal for Halifax, Nova Scotia. As the family boarded their ship, they were unaware of the German interest in Nova Scotia. The Nafthals couldn't imagine what waited for them, but when they finally arrived in Halifax, they found a seaport city with a modest urban feel and a unique mixture of the old and new architecture. Halifax boasted some impressive landmarks with notable public buildings, new large hotels, and beautiful Victorian parks and greens. The highlight of the city was the new Capitol Theatre on Barrington Street.

The family stayed in Halifax for a few days, registering at the luxurious Lord Nelson Hotel. They explored the city and became acquainted with the Baron de Hirsch Orthodox Synagogue. As they explored, they talked about their future. Max and Felix would each purchase a farm, and Sally would live with Liza and Max for the time being.

The Nafthals finally boarded a train owned and operated by the historic Dominion Atlantic Railway. It was time to travel to their last stop — the Annapolis Valley. The valley was well known for its apple orchards, farms, lumber industry and beautiful countryside. The train carried them west 64 miles (102 km), to Kentville, Kings County, one of the few prosperous communities in the valley, thanks in large part to the railway. Kentville was especially popular as a tourist destination, with its famous Cornwallis Inn located in the town centre.

The family stepped off the train in Kentville on a hot summer day unlike any they had ever encountered. They had finally arrived in rural eastern Canada.

Liza had rented a short-term apartment — an unfurnished suite located above the Dominion Grocery Store. Liza, Max, Sally and Vera all stood looking at one another for some time after they'd arrived.

The family's own furniture and possessions were on route, or so they hoped. In the meantime, Liza set up old crates for tables and dressers. She purchased a few pieces of garden furniture and put mattresses on the floor for their beds. The apartment did not come with a fridge, so they bought blocks of ice from the store downstairs. Thanks to the extreme heat that summer, the ice promptly melted in its cardboard boxes.

After so many losses, weeks of travel, and now severe homesickness, the adults went into complete shock. They were not prepared for their new lives, for the waves of emotion — or the intensity of their grief. Max had an especially difficult time; he wanted to go home and complained constantly. Even after hearing Europe's horrific news, Max's griping did not stop.

Liza and Max felt alone in their new environment and helpless to stop what was happening in Europe. They worried about the family and friends they'd left behind. There was no one outside the family to talk to about their pain and confusion. What the adults needed was time to adapt to their new rural lives. After all, the family had made a seven-year commitment to Canadian Immigration.

Everything was strange in the new country, even the food. In contrast with the adults, Vera was thrilled with her new home. She didn't care about the differences in Canada; she was having a glorious time. She soon discovered that Mutti and Vati would refuse her nothing.

From the beginning, Vera made it clear how she felt about their new life. What did food and furniture matter? There was so much to see and learn in this new, wonderful world. Vera didn't want to waste a single minute worrying about what came next. She woke up happy every day, eager to discover something new and exciting. The very best part of their situation was that they were free. Liza was soon in agreement with her daughter, and her anxiety quickly disappeared. After all, Liza had achieved just what she'd wanted — her family was safe. It was time to start their new lives.

Liza was also secretly relieved for her daughter. Vera's newfound happiness appeared to overshadow her recent fears and horrific memories. In 1939, in rural Nova Scotia, there were no professional therapists to deal with such trauma and loss. It was expected that one would forget the horrors of the past, and move on with life. From the perspective of the outside world, the family did just that.

Like her mother, Vera was quick to pick up new English words. It became a game of speaking broken English to her mother and German to her father in the same conversation.

Poor Max was another story. He had always been a social man, and now he felt isolated and lonely. Max couldn't speak or read a word of English, which meant that he couldn't learn the European news firsthand. He missed long conversations and exhilarating debates with his friends and family. He missed his work, his employees and his customers. Max quickly became bored and homesick, wishing he had never come to Canada. Liza was convinced war in Europe was imminent, and she was determined to wait out that pending war. Max refused to believe it would get that far.

Something was needed to lift Max's spirits, and Liza decided English lessons would be just the thing. She hired a tutor for her husband, a young law student named Webster McDonald who was studying at Acadia University in Wolfville, just 9 miles (14 km) west of Kentville. As in Max's youth, the traditional style of teaching did not work. Although he was still miserable, the lessons continued.

While Webster visited the apartment several times a week, Liza and Vera went out for walks to give the men privacy. Learning English seemed an impossible task for Max, but he was in luck. Webster needed a well-paying job, and this motivated him to find a way to teach his student by focusing on Max's love of music and song. One evening Liza and Vera were walking back to the apartment, when they heard singing. Max's first music lesson in English was *God Save the King*, which he bellowed out at the top of his lungs. Then came *Oh Canada,* followed by *My Bonnie Lies Over the Ocean*. And so, it continued.

Thanks to Webster, Max slowly learned the English language with a fairly strong European accent. His understanding of the spoken language came first. His speech and reading slowing improved, and he got by quite nicely. The English lessons opened up a whole new world for Max, and he blossomed beyond all Canada's expectations.

---

I wonder again about my grandfather and his learning challenges. It was extremely difficult for Grampy to learn English — and his learning shows how desperate he was to succeed in his new adopted country.

Looking at my own situation with a short-term memory impairment and using special learning techniques, I still couldn't learn a new language. I know, I've tried several times without success. I am extremely impressed and proud of my grandfather and his achievements in learning English while under a great deal of stress during his early days in Canada.

Chapter 36

# The Farm

> We looked to buy a farm with my Uncle Sally, who stayed with us for a number of years. We were shown farms by an agent of the CPR, who was also an interpreter for us. The farms shown to us were rundown, poor, and not at all what my father and mother were used to. Then one day somebody mentioned the S.S. Stevens place to Vati. We went to look at it, and it was love at first sight with him. The house was huge - way too big for us. The farm had many buildings and the barn was enormous, but my dad loved it till the day he died.
>
> -VERA OLGA (NAFTHAL) GOLDSTON

**Purchasing a farm was** not an easy task. Liza and Max began to have second thought about their commitment to Canada, and quickly became discouraged with both the properties and the agent. They were especially shocked at the countless shabby outhouses. "Surely a good, sound house with indoor plumbing isn't too much to ask," insisted Max.

One day an acquaintance in Montreal told Max about the S.S. Stevens' place. It was situated in Nictaux, which in Mi'kmsaq means *'the forks of the rivers.'* The property overlooked the Nictaux River, nestled between the North and South Mountains of the Annapolis Valley, just under 2.5 miles (4 km) from the town of Middleton.

The approximately 1,000-acre property was originally built and operated as a private hunting and fishing lodge by a group of wealthy Americans. When the lodge was sold, it became a successful working farm, with beef cattle, horses, chickens, barns, pastures and apple orchards. A large chicken coop was added, and a coopery produced the orchard's apple barrels.

The agent drove Liza, Max, Sally and Vera to Nictaux, turning off Highway 10 onto Highway 201 at the tiny United Church. The family's hopes rose instantly the moment they saw the Stevens' place. They drove past an apple orchard laden with fruit, then turned onto a circular driveway, passing a large garden on the right and a long, low chicken coop on the left. The vehicle finally came to a stop behind the main house, and the family piled out of the car. They looked around in amazement. Beyond the chicken coop were barns for beef cattle, outbuildings, two smaller houses for farmhands, and land farther than the eye could see.

Max turned and looked at the house. The huge, shingled home was painted rusty-red with white trim, to match the farm buildings. The house had an enormous, sloping roof, and plenty of windows to let in the sun. The veranda ran one hundred and twenty-five feet around two full sides of the house. In short, the well-maintained farm was grand — although the house was far larger than they needed. Liza, Max and Vera all smiled at one another and walked into the home.

In the living room, they stared at the beautiful stone fireplace surrounded by walls with rich walnut paneling. The dark hardwood floors felt solid under their feet. They moved into the spacious dining room and walked over to the large picture windows overlooking a pasture.

On the right was a road leading to a bridge across the Nictaux River. Liza and Max were impressed — but they were also practical. Max flushed every toilet in the house. As the family wandered from room to room, they opened cupboard doors and flicked light switches on and off. The place felt like home.

Max was instantly in love with the property. For the first time, the thought of being a farmer appealed to him. Max and Liza looked at each other, smiled and nodded. Their offer was accepted. The Nafthals had found their new home and farm.

Max's brother Felix, soon acquired a small farm as well. It was located on Route 201 in the rural community of Round Hill, halfway between the valley market towns of Bridgetown and Annapolis Royal, and about 22 miles (36 km) west of Nictaux.

---

Like my grandfather, I have always loved the farm. I still do — to this day. Even after the farm was sold, as a child I would ride my bike the 4 km back to Nictaux. I'd cycle past the main house and ride down the road a way; then I'd turn around, pass the farm, heading back to town and home again.

Chapter 37

# Religion and the Baron de Hirsch Synagogue

> We were shocked - some people in the Jewish community spoke Yiddish, a broken slang deriving from German. Out of respect for the European Jews, Mutti refused to ever speak a word of Yiddish again, so this was not a good start with the western synagogue. Mutti had no tolerance when it came to her expectations of the Jews, and neither did I. What had religion ever done for us? Nothing. Vati was another story; he was raised an Orthodox Jew and needed to be attached to the synagogue no matter what. So we made it work.
>
> -VERA OLGA (NAFTHAL) GOLDSTON

**The Nafthal's Jewish background** was common knowledge in their adopted community, although most residents knew nothing about the Jewish faith or practices. This was fine with the family; they were low-key about their religion and just worked hard to fit into the community. In fact, Liza was not as religious as Max, nor did she encourage Vera when it came to the "nonsense of religion."

She was quick to voice her opinion; "What did religion ever give me, but grief?"

Vera was exposed to the Orthodox beliefs and traditional holidays through her father and beloved grandfather, Wolfe. Liza went along with this. Still, it was not surprising that Vera shared her mother's opinions. What had religion ever done for them?

Unlike Liza, Max was born and raised an Orthodox Jew. He was brought up in a kosher home. His father, Wolfe, was an Orthodox Jew, as well as the loyal housekeeper who helped raise Max and his siblings. Max's religious roots ran deep; he needed his people and faith more than ever before. The closest synagogue was in Halifax, 95.7 miles (153 km) away.

Liza's rationale didn't work for Max. In part, he agreed with his wife — so much horror and so many losses. And over what — religion? But he was unwilling to give up his spiritual beliefs, and so instead he became a prominent member of the Orthodox Baron de Hirsch Synagogue in Halifax.

The distance between the synagogue and the farm suited Liza and Vera. They wanted to fit into their new community — and a synagogue did not fit into rural life.

The family did not get off to a good start. They were shocked to find many residents in the Jewish community speaking a form of Yiddish. Since Yiddish is a Germanic dialect, once the family left their homeland, they agreed never to speak this language again. Nothing prepared them for this — especially Liza. She felt the community had no respect or understanding for European Jews.

Liza insisted western Jews were nothing like European Jews. They seemed disconnected from their roots and did not follow the traditional Orthodox laws. But Liza understood that Max needed to be associated with a temple, and so she supported her husband's decision. Although it was always Max who suggested going to shul,[85] Liza and Vera would often go along.

That first Saturday Liza was upset by what she observed. The orthodox law states that no one should work on the Jewish Sabbath,[86] and that extends to driving a vehicle. But the synagogue was too far away, and so the family had no choice but to travel by car — which Liza accepted because of the circumstances. Out of respect, Max parked their vehicle several blocks from the synagogue, and then the family walked the remaining blocks to the front steps of the temple. What infuriated Liza was that the family had lots of company along the way. Most of the synagogue's members drove to Saturday shul — even members who lived close by. Liza was quick to point out that this practice would *not* happen in Europe. Max, in contrast, was forgiving. After all, he had driven too. And so — it continued.

Max and Liza made friends in the small Jewish community — although they were mostly friends of Max! The couple was very popular and often entertained members of the synagogue in their beautiful country home. Their friends loved leaving the city to enjoy the Nafthal's wonderful European hospitality out in the country. They especially enjoyed Liza's fabulous French/Canadian cuisine. Vera and Max often laughed at Liza because she complained about the Jewish community, but she still loved to dress up in her pretty clothes and wear her jewelry for any social religious event.

Max accepted the Baron de Hirsch community's differences. He didn't care because he loved his Jewish roots and continued to be a prominent and active member of the Halifax temple until his death. After Max's passing, Liza and Vera did not support or attend the synagogue again.

---

My grandmother claimed the European Jews were truer to their authentic roots than the small Halifax Jewish community. Jews in North America were exposed to a degree of anti-Semitism, but it was not as horrifying as the anti-Semitism experienced by the Jews in Europe —because of this, my grandmother felt they had a lack of understanding and respect for the European Jews. I was always aware that Nanny and Mom had no tolerance for the difference between European Jews and some Western Jews.

---

In the spring of 2018, a book belonging to Adolf Hitler was purchased by Library and Archives Canada (LAC). The book is entitled *Statistik, Presse und Organisation des Judentums in den Vereinigten Staaten und Kanada* (*Statistics, Media and Organizations of Jewry in the United States and Canada*). On the inside cover is a bookplate with the name Adolf Hitler, evidence the book belonged to him. The bookplate also includes an eagle, oak leaf, and swastika, all symbols of the Nazi Party. After liberation, the book was taken from his private collection at Hitler's vacation home near Berchtesgaden in the Bavarian Alps.

The 137-page book, commissioned by the Nazis, was written by Heinz Kloss. Kloss was a researcher and worked for organizations that supported the Third Reich. He lived in the United States during the pre-war years, 1936-1937. The book contains details of the Jewish population and organizations in both the U.S. and Canada.

Kloss had collected the names of Canadian Jews in both large and small communities, including Nova Scotia. The book was to be used in the Nazi 'Final Solution' — their plan to eliminate all Jews worldwide.[87]

Liza, Max and Vera arrived in Canada in 1939 — they wouldn't be on the list. The family, however, would have been easy to find because they were registered as members of the Baron de Hirsch Synagogue — which was listed in the book. If the outcome of WWII had been different, Canada would have fallen under the Nazi Regime. All Jewish Canadians would be in trouble.

Chapter 38

# Starting Over

> Back to the farm now. We moved in September, at last our furniture had come and it was good to have the old familiar comfort around us again. Vati was happy now, the big shot farmer. Everyone was his best friend again.
>
> -VERA OLGA (NAFTHAL) GOLDSTON

THE FAMILY HAD BEEN in Canada less than two months, when WWII was declared on September 1, 1939. From the moment war was announced, Max stopped griping about returning to Europe. Just like that, the family no longer had to put up with Max's grumpiness. Instead, Max and the family worried constantly about their families and friends in Europe.

On that same day, Liza and Max's CPR agent and interpreter was arrested for being a Nazi spy. The German Reich's long reach extended to Canada — all the way to the Nafthal's front door. Liza and Max wondered if they would ever truly be safe.

In late September 1939, Liza, Max, Vera and Sally moved into their new home. Max loved the land from the beginning. With something to finally keep him busy, he quickly took over management of the farm. Life was bittersweet as the family settled into their new surroundings while the news from Europe worsened.

Shortly before their move into the farmhouse, Liza received notification that their furniture and possessions had finally arrived. It felt wonderful to have some of their familiar belongings. Dinner tasted better at their dining room table. Beautiful paintings were hung, furniture put in place, and the linens and silver organized. Every night, the family fell asleep exhausted from work and worry, but content in their warm, comfortable beds. Liza could not help herself — she often ran her hands across the dark oak furniture and slipped her fingers into the soft, rich folds of the linens. Sometimes she would stop what she was doing just to touch one of the beautiful objects that gave her comfort. Although, their new community was small, Liza never complained. In fact, everything was just as she'd hoped and more.

Middleton was their main centre for mail, banking and supplies. The biggest contributor to the town's economy was the Royal Canadian Airforce Base, located in Greenwood, Kings County, 6 miles (10 km) east of Middleton. A few locals blamed the absence of a growing economy on the town's politicians. For decades the town council had opposed change — and that had worked, since most residents liked Middleton just the way it was.

The town sat at the halfway point between Halifax and the seaside community of Yarmouth, on the beautiful south shore. Middleton, known as the 'Heart of the Valley,' was situated in the valley centre on the north banks of the Annapolis River. In late 1939, Middleton was a quaint little town with a population of about 1,700 residents.

The downtown consisted of two intersecting streets. The small shops on either side of Commercial Street included Stedman's Department Store, modelled after the old 'Five & Dime,' a small drug store, a grocer's and a shoe store. The Royal Bank of Canada was an impressive brick building located on the corner of Commercial and Main Streets. Main Street ran in a straight east-to-west line right through town. The Maritime Telephone & Telegraph Co (MT&T) was a striking wooden structure on Main. Across the street from the telephone company was the Middleton Post Office, while up the street was the popular Capitol Theatre, which featured a weekly movie. The town also had a few much-loved greasy spoon restaurants.

West of town on Gates Street stood the grey-shingled Soldiers Memorial Hospital. If things did not work out in the hospital, Roop's Funeral Home was available! Further west of town, McKenzie's Creamery made fresh butter and delicious ice cream. Near the creamery, the Scotian Gold Plant processed much of the valley's abundant fruits and vegetables.

The Dominion Atlantic Railway started in 1917, and rolled through Middleton from Halifax, travelling as far south as Yarmouth. You could hear the train's whistle all over town. The engine would slow at railway crossings; the whistle blew, and then blew again as it arrived at the old train station. A wooden plaque with MIDDLETON printed in large white letters welcomed travellers.

While the town was a far cry from Paris or London, it had nearly everything a person might need. And if not, there was always Halifax. While the news in Europe worsened, Liza, Max and Vera built strong, loving bonds with their new community. They tried hard not to show their worry and stress, but others could see the new residents were enduring difficult times.

On September 10, 1939, the Canadian government made an official declaration — Canada was at war with Germany. Nova Scotia exploded with the wartime industry.

That fall, Liza found a chilling photograph among their belongings. It was a photo of Max in full German uniform during WWI. She showed the picture to her husband, and he was extremely upset. Max did not need a reminder that he'd been forced into the German army as a young man. What made matters worse, is the photograph brought up memories of his commander demanding he fight his fellow Lithuanians. Max was afraid the image would be discovered and bring the family to ruins. Without another word, he tossed the photograph into the fireplace. Liza was glad to see the last of the photo as well.

As the war raged in Europe, Max discovered that he loved being a landowner. He managed the property with enthusiasm, hiring permanent farmworkers who moved into the small cottages on the property. When necessary, Max easily found local seasonal workers as well. The farm flourished, and Max brought much-needed employment to rural Annapolis Valley. At first, the workers were leery of the family from away, but jobs were hard to find. Max took a great personal interest in his employees and showed his appreciation for their hard work. It didn't take long for word to get out. Max built his reputation in his new country the same way he had built it in his homeland — with his jolly personality, his genuine interest in people, and his endless generosity. Soon the locals loved Max. Once again everyone was his best friend. He was happy.

Life was changing for Vera too. Liza enrolled her daughter in Middleton MacDonald Consolidated School,[88] with classes from primary through grade twelve. The school was an impressive two-story brick building, with wide wooden stairs leading up to large double front doors. Every inch of the school, from the basement to the attic, was used for education.

Attending MacDonald School in Canada was the next phase of Vera's great adventure. She gladly left her parents and the farm, enjoying her new independence.

Liza was busy reinventing herself too. She quickly discovered a use for her 'Le Cordon Bleu' culinary skills. The farmhands' compensation included a hot noontime meal, and coffee with baked snacks during the day. The women of the farm always provided these meals. Liza, who'd never cooked for anyone in her life, reinvented herself as the farm's 'chief cook and bottle washer.'

She quickly learned to cook the noontime meals, bake cookies and pies, and produce rich cups of coffee for working men's hearty appetites. The prestigious Le Cordon Bleu did not train chefs to feed wholesome meals to hard-working farmhands — but what did that matter to Liza? At first, her lack of experience put her nerves on edge; Liza worried her training would not satisfy a famished group of labourers. She was so mistaken. With the help of a few of the farmhands' wives, Liza developed a hearty European/North American flair for meals and baked goods that the men loved. As her confidence grew, her creativity was endless. Liza was now cooking for the farmhands, friends and family.

Liza welcomed the demands of the kitchen, never once complaining. Cooking kept her mind occupied, and for that she was glad. Whenever possible, Liza used their poultry, beef and fresh produce. Her warm kitchen was filled with the aromas of roasting meats, steaming vegetables and fresh fruit pies. Her soups, gravies and sauces were beyond imagination. The wonderful smells poured out the kitchen's screened door, onto the veranda and through the yard — enticing any workers who might be close by.

Liza traded her fashionable European clothes for simple, fitted cotton dresses, and her silk stockings for bare legs. Yet somehow, Liza always retained her beauty, style and elegance. If only her old friends and family could be with her now. They would all have a good laugh together, working beside Liza without complaint. Liza's busy kitchen was paradise compared to the horrors taking place in Europe.

---

In mid-August 1939, while the family were preparing to move to the farm, the German Consul General to Canada asked to borrow the British High Commissioner's maps. He explained that he had orders from Berlin to tour the Maritime Provinces. In the end, Germany withdrew the request.[89]

In November 1939, Canadian military intelligence reported that German shortwave radio broadcasts had revealed the number of ships departing in convoy from Halifax Harbour. Fortunately — this was not public information. While I'm grateful that my family likely never knew of this development, today I find the information chilling.

Chapter 39

# Telegrams

> Telegrams came from Europe begging for help to escape, but alas it was too late. Vati tried, but it was hopeless right from the start.
>
> -VERA OLGA (NAFTHAL) GOLDSTON

**Shortly after the war** began, as the Jews of Memel and Lithuania struggled to find refuge in South Africa, the United States and Canada, telegrams arrived at the farm from both sides of the family, and friends as well.

*"PLEASE. CAN YOU HELP? NEED TO LEAVE EUROPE ASAP!"*

*"CONDITIONS WORSENED. CAN YOU HELP AT YOUR END?"*

*"NAZIS ARE A PROBLEM FOR THE JEWS. ASK IF THERE IS HELP?"*

Liza and Max were devastated as the news worsened. On September 28, 1939, Poland's capital was brutally seized by the Nazis. Liza's sister Mania, brother Grisha, and their families all lived in Poland.

Max's brother Bernard and his family still lived in Hanover, Germany. His older brother Nathan and his family lived in Kaunas, Lithuania. By now, Max's sister, Hannah, and her family had left Memel for Kaunas too. The actual locations of their many extended relatives on both sides of the family were unknown. Liza and Max worked tirelessly with Canadian Immigration to find a way out for their family members and friends, but this was an extremely complicated process.

The Nazis considered Jewish Memelland citizenships to be expendable. New passports and exit visas were impossible to obtain, and all neighbouring land borders were closed to the Jewish people. The only other route out of Lithuania was Memel Harbour on the Baltic Sea, still closed to Jews as well. Most Memel Jews had relocated to Kaunas, but the city was also crowded with immigrants from Germany, Austria and the Czechoslovak Republic. The Jewish people were trapped.[90]

Desperate telegrams continued to arrive.

*"OUR HOMES AND BUSINESSES ARE CONFISCATED. LIVING IN A GHETTO. SEE WHAT YOU CAN DO?"*

*"JEWS ARRESTED FOR NO REASON AND NEVER SEEN AGAIN. IS HELP POSSIBLE ON YOUR END?"*

Fearful that their families would disappear forever, Liza and Max continued to work with Canadian authorities. Until one horrible day — they had to face the truth — it was too late for the Jews in Europe. There was no hope of getting anyone out.

Liza and Max kept updated with war events through local newspapers and radio, but of course, television and the internet did not yet exist. The Canadian government placed restrictions on the news distributed to the public during the war. Freedom of information disappeared. What remained was a watered-down version of events, which only delayed the news of the Holocaust's horrors.

Liza and Max were struck another painful blow when the telegrams stopped coming. Trapped behind borders, their European family members went completely silent, disappearing without a trace. This silence would haunt Liza, Max and Vera for the rest of their lives. They were determined to move ahead through their days, but their European family was never far from their thoughts. The worry was constant.

---

My grandparents and mother loved Canada. I never once heard them mention a bad word about their adopted country. They believed this was the best place in the world to live and especially loved Nova Scotia and its residents. "You can go anywhere in the world," my mother once told me, "But you'll always be glad to come home to Nova Scotia." Years later, I discovered this to be true.

---

In 1939, Bruce Jefferson, a Halifax journalist and newspaper editor was appointed Regional Censor of Publications. He was responsible for reviewing all wartime news material for publication or broadcast and advising editors and producers. Jefferson decided what could and could not be shared with the public in sixteen daily newspapers, sixty-eight weeklies and ten radio stations across the Atlantic Provinces. While the European news was horrific, not even Jefferson was aware of the worst. The Nazis successfully hid the slow starvation, horrific torture and mass murders taking place in their concentration and death camps.[91] During wartime, my grandparents never knew of the true devastation, and perhaps it was better that way.

Chapter 40

# Settling In

> Vati was happy now, the big shot farmer!
>
> -VERA OLGA (NAFTHAL) GOLDSTON

**Vera thought it was** hilarious to watch Mutti work her way around the kitchen, with its big pots of potatoes, great slabs of beef, and whole chickens waiting to be stuffed by Mutti and the housekeeper. Every day, cookies came out of the oven on oversized pans. Each cookie Mutti made was identical in size and shape. Not so with the housekeeper's baking; she would look at Mutti's cookies and shake her head in disbelief.

A favourite European cookie of Vera's was the *Hallongrotta*, known by Canadians as a thumbprint cookie. A thumbprint is made in the middle of a round vanilla cookie and filled with jam before baking. In Europe, these cookies were tiny, served with tea, coffee or milk. In Canada, however, they were the size of Vera's palm. This impressed the girl, especially when fieldhands ate the cookies in one gulp, then went for a second, third and fourth helping. Mutti watched the men in shock at first, until she realized it was a tribute to her baking skills and encouraged the men to eat more.

Vera also had fun observing Vati's new zest for life on the farm. When the family lived in Europe, Vati had always travelled for business. Vera was thrilled to have her father working so close to home almost every day.

Vati's previous experience gave him a strong foundation for operating any business — even the farm. He was a curious man, with a gift for making solid decisions. Max understood people and their characters. He hired an experienced foreman and the right workers to help him learn the farming business. His effective management resulted in a low turnover of workers and a better yield of crops and livestock, which meant increased production and profitability. Like Mutti's cooking, Vati's farming was hard work, but it came easily to him. Perhaps Mutti and Vati were in survivor mode, or perhaps they needed to throw themselves into their new lives to help deal with their worries.

For her part, Vera was happy on the farm, especially watching her parents recreate themselves. In Europe, Vera called her father 'the big shot.' Now she called him 'the big shot farmer.' Everyone laughed, but Max would stand taller and pull his shoulders back. He was proud of his nickname.

Chapter 41

# School Days

**Vera loved learning. Every** morning she looked forward to Vati driving her to the local school. While most of the students accepted her, some were not as welcoming as others and called her mean names, like 'kike.' Referring to a person of the Jewish faith, the word is extremely offensive. A few children also mimicked her strong Memelland accent — Vera never could pronounce a 'w.'

The bullying came to the attention of the principal, Mr. D.B. Wright. One day he called out to Vera as she was passing his open office door. She was surprised but knew she had done nothing wrong. Pulling her shoulders back, she walked into the office and sat down in the seat offered to her.

Mr. Wright went by the rules, and for that, he was not a well-liked principal among the student body. But Vera didn't know Mr. Wright, and since she was not a girl who followed the crowd, she had no opinion one way or the other. For a few minutes, the two sat in silence, occasionally looking at each other. Then Mr. Wright laid down his pen and smiled at Vera.

"How are you making out in school, Vera?"

"Good. I like school!"

"Are you happy here with us?"

"Of course!"

"And how are you getting along with the other students?" Mr. Wright asked.

"Good."

"Are you making friends?"

"Friends? Yes."

"I understand that some of the students are calling you names," Mr. Wright said, looking straight at Vera.

Vera didn't understand and stared back at Mr. Wright.

"The name-calling. Do you understand what this means?"

"Yes, the name-calling," said Vera. "I understand what the words mean."

"This is wrong, Vera. You can always come to me."

"What? Why would I come to you?" Vera asked.

"To put a stop to this! It won't be happening in my school anymore!" the principal said with unexpected fury. Vera straightened and blinked several times at Mr. Wright's tone. In that same instant, Vera realized he wanted to protect her feelings.

"Mr. Wright, in my country, people called me those names and worse. I was frightened. But they do not bother me in Canada."

"Why don't they frighten you here?" asked Mr. Wright.

"Because it is just name-calling, nothing else! After all, their words cannot kill me. In Europe, I could have been murdered," Vera informed the shocked and red-faced principal. From that moment on, Vera always adored Mr. Wright.[92]

---

Mr. D.B. Wright was not remembered as a popular principal. He demanded the best from his students and believed respect and compassion were crucial — but he was also a rigid rule enforcer. Mom adored him from that first meeting, until his death years later. She admitted it bothered her that people did not feel the same way about this wonderful man.

My older sister Janet recently shared Mr. D.B. Wright's story with me. It was the first time I'd heard it, and it horrified me. For days, I agonized over other students calling my mother terrible names. I was shocked that these children could act so cruelly towards a young girl — a girl who had already lived through so much persecution.

By the time I was ready to begin my education, the Middleton MacDonald Consolidated School went from grade primary (the equivalent of kindergarten) to grade six. Like my mother, my name was added to the enrollment list.

This was normal practice for rural living — many of my friends' parents had attended the same school. Most of them seemed to be around my mother's age. Could some of these parents be the same students who had mocked my mother and called her terrible names? I thought back to my childhood friends and their parents. "Did *she* call Mom names? Did *he*?" I knew one of them must be guilty, maybe more than one. Not many people left Middleton in those days, and not many new families moved in.

And I had questions. Where had these rural children learned such ugly names? We lived in a small community — where they still living in Middleton? If so, did Mom speak to them. Were they friends now? My head was spinning! Was Mom reminded of the name-calling when she saw my friends? Did anyone ever apologize to Mom? I was going mad!

Mom's experience with name-calling in our hometown left me with another mystery. Then I remembered the childhood rhyme — *Sticks and stones can break my bones, but names will never hurt me.*

Mom was safe and free; she was grateful for the protection Canada provided and the opportunity to live her life. I finally understood my mother's way of thinking. Nothing else mattered.

Chapter 42

# Vera's Gratitude

> Mutti often told me I was a very smart girl. She said, "Lucky for you, you have my brains when it comes to studies, and not your father's difficulties with learning.
>
> -VERA OLGA (NAFTHAL) GOLDSTON

**As a young child,** Vera had lots to worry about, but her 'get over it quick' attitude helped her bury her anxiety. Like her parents, aunts and uncles, Vera internalized everything. Her outward appearance gave the impression of a well-adjusted child.

Canada continued to be Vera's greatest adventure. She loved the countryside and the people. She never compared the bustling cities of London or Paris to the quaint town of Middleton. Vera was thrilled to be attending Middleton MacDonald Consolidated School, and learning was a breeze.

Life was simpler on the farm, and Vera's gratitude for Canada ran deep. The dreadful fear of anti-Semitism was largely a thing of the past — at least for the immediate family. Vera felt secretly guilty when she thought of her friends and family back in Europe, but she did her best to shake this guilt off quickly and move on with her life. There were no other options.

At home, Vera spoke English with her mother and German with her father, until his English improved. She was also fluent in German, Russian, French and Yiddish, but there were no opportunities to use these languages in Eastern Canada. Vera's only exceptions were the German names for mother and father — Mutti and Vati.

"You're a very smart girl," Mutti often told her daughter. "Lucky for you, you have my brains when it comes to studies, and not your father's difficulties with learning." On these occasions, father and daughter would look at each other, and Vati would send a secret wink. Vera loved being in cahoots with her father, whom she believed to be the kindest and most intelligent man in the world. Still, when it came to studying, she was secretly thankful she had Mutti's brains.

Vera quickly climbed the ranks to the honour roll at school and maintained her high marks throughout her studies. She discovered a love for science and spent endless hours in the lab, located in the attic of the schoolhouse. One day, Vera and two boys almost blew up the school. The smoke bomb they created smelled so rotten, that all four floors, from the basement to the attic, had to be evacuated. Secretly, Vati and Vera thought the whole event was very funny, but Mutti was furious. Vera's plans for the future were set — she would go to university to become a scientist.

Chapter 43

# Christmas and New Friends

**Sally was happy on** the farm with Liza, Max and Vera, while Felix and Lottie were content on their farm in Round Hill.

Meanwhile, Liza, Max and Vera were meeting many local Nictaux and Middleton residents. Tom and Peg Hankinson and their daughter, Dianne, lived in Middleton, and the two men quickly realized they were a perfect match. Tom was the owner of the Valley Milling Company, a local lumber business, and he introduced Max to all his colleagues in Nova Scotia's timber industry. The two families quickly became great friends, enjoying many happy times together. Max and Liza trusted Tom and Peg. They shared their stories about Liza and Vera fleeing to France, and Max's narrow escape out of Memel. They also shared their worries and grief for their European family and spoke of the horrors of the ghettos and camps.[93] It was good to have friends who listened. Liza and Max's roots in Nova Scotia were growing ever deeper.

In late 1939, as the Christmas season drew near, Max wondered what all the excitement was about. It didn't take long for the joy of the holiday to capture his heart. Liza and Max talked about their need to fit into their community — recognizing that Christian holidays were a huge part of the local culture. They didn't see Christmas as a religious celebration, but a season filled with reasons to celebrate and spoil the people they loved. Liza and Max quickly adopted Christmas, doing it up in grand style. They loved shopping, giving beautifully-wrapped gifts, and hosting huge feasts for family and friends. They always remembered the employees and their families with gifts, large turkeys and crates of fresh oranges. The glow of Christmas lights, tinsel and wonderful new friends brightened their lives and gave them some peace for a short period of time.

---

I wanted to find someone who knew my grandparents in the early days on the farm. This was not an easy task, given that eighty years had passed — but it wasn't impossible. I began my search and found an article written by Dianne Hankinson LeGard in the September 28, 2008, issue of the *Aurora Newspaper*, in Greenwood, Nova Scotia. The article included a memory involving my grandparents and their farm. I easily found Dianne, and she happily shared warm memories of my grandparents and her many visits to the farm. Dianne fondly remembers the strong bond between her father and my grandfather. She recalled my grandfather often dropping in for a visit at their home or her dad's office at the Valley Milling Company.

Dianne and her parents spent many Christmases at the farm. She remembers one special Christmas when Liza and Max gave her a picture of cats that shone in the dark. If she woke in the middle of the night, this picture brought her peace; it was as though the cats were keeping watch over her. Eighty years later, Dianne still has that picture.[94]

One day, Dianne sent me a lovely note. She wrote, "I want you to know that the Nafthal family was very well-liked and respected by the local people. The family may have been forced to leave their former lives behind, but they brought a European flair and sophistication to their new life in Nictaux." [95] Dianne's note still brings tears to my eyes.

---

Grampy loved Christmas with a passion. Mom once told me Grampy was so excited about Christmas, that he couldn't wait for it to arrive. His love for shopping would take him on spending sprees while he was in Montreal on business. He'd come home loaded with gifts, but he could never wait until the holidays to give the presents to his grandchildren. Then he'd have to shop for Christmas all over again!

Chapter 44

# The Nafthal's Hospitality

**Nova Scotia was consumed** with wartime activity. The farm was situated just 8 miles (13 km) from the Royal Canadian Air Force (RCAF) Station in Greenwood. While the base may have appeared misplaced in the rural farmlands of Nova Scotia, the area was known for its relatively fog-free climate, a critical element for an air force base.

During WWII, the farm's proximity to Greenwood meant blackout periods. Blackout curtains were installed in the farm's main house, two cottages and outbuildings. By September 4, 1939, parts of Nova Scotia were experiencing their first air raid blackouts, which continued throughout the war.

The Greenwood base was a significant contributor to the war effort. On December 17, 1939, an official agreement was signed between the RCAF Base Greenwood and the British Commonwealth Air Training Plan (BCATP). By March 9, 1942, the first training units from the United Kingdom, Australia and New Zealand arrived. Canadian training facilities supplied the majority of aircrew for overseas operational services. During the war, one hundred and thirty thousand aircrews trained for overseas fighting on the Greenwood base.[96]

It quickly became evident that the base was too small to accommodate all the airmen. A request went out to surrounding communities for housing for the men and their families. Liza and Max immediately offered the full upstairs of their stately home to Royal Air Force (RAF) officers and their families. The RAF officers and their families soon filled the large home. Liza, Max and Vera were surrounded by people again.

Greenwood's isolated location did not prevent the men from becoming war casualties. Airmen stationed at the base were killed, some overseas, and some during their training. One airman fondly remembered by the community was Squadron Leader Richard Arthur Miles, DFC (Distinguished Flying Cross), as well as his spotted dog, Jock. Richard flew his plane from England to Greenwood with Jock in the cockpit. Both the airman and the dog moved into the Nafthal home and quickly became part of the family. In December 1942, Richard's wife and young daughter joined him for Christmas at the Nafthal residence. They remained there until the spring of 1943 when Richard was killed in a plane crash in a wooded area near Auburn, Nova Scotia. This accident devastated the Nafthals and the community. Richard's pregnant wife and daughter returned to England, while Jock, the spotted dog, was given to Dianne Hankinson, the daughter of family friends. Jock became a lasting and happy reminder of Richard and his family. In August 1943, the family received a birth announcement for Richard's son, Hugh Miles.[97]

Many single men, some of them Jewish, arrived weekly at the Greenwood base. Most of these airmen were away from home for the first time. The airmen lived in tight quarters as they trained for war. The Nafthals saw this as another opportunity to help the war effort. In appreciation for the servicemen's dedication, Liza and Max opened their doors wider, welcoming Jewish airmen to their home every weekend and holiday.

The Jewish Shabbat[98] begins on Friday at sundown with a festive dinner and ends on Saturday at sundown when the third star appears in the sky. Every Friday afternoon, and on all Jewish and Christian holidays, Max would drive to the base. He extended an open invitation to any Jewish airmen who wanted to exchange their crowded bunks and meals at the mess for a welcome break. The servicemen were more than happy to come. Most locals welcomed the airmen into their homes, but there was little opportunity for the Jewish soldiers to spend time in Jewish homes.

The dynamic Nafthals' warm European hospitality, the company of their good friends, plus Liza's popular cuisine quickly became a favourite with the airmen arriving at the door with overnight bags and rumbling stomachs. They were welcomed with open arms and a festive atmosphere. Liza did not always know how many men would show up for the Shabbat dinner, but the dining room was quickly set to accommodate additional guests — and there was always plenty of food for everyone. Under the dark shadow of war, the farm brought comfort and cheer to everyone who visited. Liza and Max would have done anything for these men.

As the war raged on, the airmen continued to appreciate their weekends and holidays with the Nafthals. In 1943, an airman named Johnny Birds invited his best friend, Joe Goldston, to join him at the farm. Joe was a handsome, young airman from Blackfriars, England, who usually kept busy on weekends in the company of a local girl from Kingston. But one weekend he found himself free and agreed to tag along with Johnny to the farm. As Max drove the two young men away from their designated meeting place, he and Joe had no idea how their lives were about to change forever.

Vera was now eighteen years old and a grade twelve honour student. A beautiful, strong-minded young woman who knew exactly what she wanted and how to get it. Vera planned to attend university and become a scientist. She always longed for the comfort of the many relatives she had loved so much as a young child, so she also wanted to marry and have a large family. When Joe walked through the front door of the farmhouse, Vera's plans for university vanished. Joe's girlfriend disappeared into the background just as quickly. And so began the amazing, lifelong love affair between beautiful Vera Olga Nafthal and handsome Corporal Joseph Henry Goldston.

Chapter 45

# Vera and Joe

**Six months passed after** Vera met Joe, and everyone could see the couple was madly in love. One evening as Vera's parents were leaving for the movies, Vera and Joe asked to speak with them. Beaming from ear to ear, they made the great announcement in English for Joe's benefit — they were getting married. Between the couple's excitement and her parents' preparations to leave the house, Mutti and Vati did not comprehend the news. They stopped for a moment to smile at their daughter and her handsome airman, and then, muttering some niceties, they walked out the door — leaving Vera and Joe shocked at their lack of response.

Once they were seated in the theatre, Max turned to his wife. "What foolishness were the kids talking about?"

After some thought, Liza realized what she'd heard. "Max, I think Vera said she was going to marry Joe!"

The couple looked at each other in shock. Impossible! Vera had plans for university, not marriage. She was still a child! They immediately left the theatre and returned home. Max had always imagined that he would be his daughter's matchmaker. He would seek out a suitable husband with a well-established career from a good, prosperous family — perhaps the son of one of his connections in Montreal.

Nothing about Joe matched the qualities they were looking for in a potential son-in-law. Joe was from Blackfriars, a poorer neighbourhood in London. He had no formal education – no promising future. What were they to do with him? Furthermore, the young man could be killed during the war. Joe was not what Vera's parents had visualized for their only child. But Liza knew her daughter well and was certain Vera was smitten by Joe's handsome looks and his cocky English attitude.

Liza and Max put up a good fight, but Vera stood her ground. She insisted Joe was extremely bright and had the potential for a good future if given the opportunity. As usual, Vera won the battle and her parents agreed to the marriage.

"At least he's Jewish," Max said, hugging his daughter. "A good start." Max could never deny Vera anything. When the war ended, Max agreed he would give Joe his opportunity.

Mother and daughter, however, had a different relationship. Vera would never completely forgive Mutti for disapproving of the man she wanted to marry. While both women remained close throughout their lives, at times there was an edge in Vera's voice when speaking to or about her mother.

On May 29, 1942, just days after her nineteenth birthday, Vera married Joe, the love of her life. It was a beautiful, traditional Jewish ceremony held at the prestigious Lord Nelson Hotel in Halifax. Shortly afterward Joe left to fight the war in Europe, while Vera stayed behind on the farm with her parents and waited for him.

Vera's plans for university were forgotten. Some of her time was now taken up knitting a colourful collection of beautifully designed woolen socks — gifts for Joe upon his return. The collection eventually grew to fill a large dresser drawer. Vera often wrote love letters to her handsome new husband and waited impatiently for his reply. She sent pictures of herself with deep red lipstick kisses and notes on the back. This beautiful love affair would continue through their lifetime.

---

After Dad returned from the war, he never again wore a pair of store-bought socks. Even in the heat of summer, he wore Mom's woolen creations. After my mother passed, the socks began to wear out. I'd often find Dad with a darning needle in hand and a rubber ball pushed up in the toe or heel of a worn sock. He'd darn the holes with loving care, wearing the socks over and over again.

Eventually, it became my job to knit my father's socks. But Mom hadn't knit these treasures from a pattern; the designs were all in her head. I remember the day Dad gave me a sock Mom had knitted and asked me to replicate it. Mom's knitting was unique. I took her work to yarn shops and asked the professionals what she had done, but no knitter could match her work. It was impossible to duplicate.

Dad never once complained, although my knitting never measured up to Mom's talented work. When I handed Dad a new pair of socks, he'd give me a little smile, turning them this way and that. I could see the sadness in his eyes as he looked for his wife's memory in his daughter's socks. The loving joy of knitting socks for my father turned into a daunting task, but I never told Dad.

Years later when Dad passed, my siblings and I had the chore of cleaning out our parents' house. No one wanted the socks I had knit for Dad, nor the few tattered leftover socks from Mom's creations. I still have a painful memory of the drawer being turned upside down, and Dad's socks falling into a cardboard box for the Salvation Army Thrift Store.

## Chapter 46

# Life Carries On

> We couldn't believe our ears. Why did we escape and so many perish? The reasons were many and hard for my father to accept. He was wealthy; he had everything he could wish for and never believed that the Germans would go as far as they did - that is into hell for six million Jews, of whom he most certainly would have been one of the first. But my mother was determined; she was strong and she had survived the Russian Revolution.
>
> -VERA OLGA (NAFTHAL) GOLDSTON

**By 1945, the Nafthal** family had been living in Canada for more than five years. On May 18, 1945, Max and Vera both received official certification under the Canadian Naturalization Act, giving them the rights of Canadian Citizens. For some unknown reason, Liza's citizenship did not come until several months later. Liza and Max's gratitude was enormous. On September 2, 1945, even greater news finally arrived.

Liza, Max and Vera heard the news blasting over the radio — the war was officially over. In the early days, after the excitement of the end of the war — the family's happiness was mixed with tears, sleepless nights and hope. Their thoughts went to their friends and family in Europe. Who was alive? Who had been murdered? Where was everyone? How long would it take to reconnect? So many questions — and no answers.

Liza and Max began hunting for their family. They wrote letters, they telegraphed agencies, they connected with immigration services — and they waited. As Max checked with officials from one agency after another, the bleakness of the situation sank in. Yet again, life was bittersweet.

One evening, shortly after the war ended, Liza, Max and Vera went to the local theatre. As they waited for the show to begin they chatted with friends and acquaintances.

The curtains drew back, the lights dimmed, the projector rolled — and the audience's attention turned to the screen. The global newsreel always played before the feature movie. As the newsreel lit up the big screen, the family learned for the first time the true Hell they had escaped. The announcer boomed; "WWII, the Holocaust War Crimes and the Liberated Jewish Prisoners." His words thundered in the small theatre, sending shockwaves through every listener — especially Liza, Max and Vera.

For the first few moments, the family didn't quite understand the horrors they were watching — but suddenly they knew! And their pain was quick and excruciatingly powerful. Heartbreaking pictures of liberated Jewish prisoners appeared in concentration camps. The scenes were terrifying. The audience fell into an eerie silence as the Jews stared out at them with blank, haunted eyes. Thin skin hung on starved skeleton forms with protruding stomachs, their pitiful bodies marked and bruised from beatings and forced labour. The sight was horrifying.

Men, women and children filled the screen. They all had crudely shaved heads and ill-fitting, dirty rags hanging on their gaunt bodies. The striped rags did nothing to protect them from the heat of the sun or the cold of night. Some wore mismatched and tattered shoes far too large for their feet, with laces and buckles missing. Others stood barefooted. They were all filthy. Many liberated prisoners still waited behind the now-powerless electric fence surrounding the concentration camp. They had no other place to go. Some clung to the fence for support, their strength was almost gone.

The camera flickered for a few seconds, making the audience blink. Then the picture came back into view, showing a mass grave in the background. The reporter pointed, holding a hanky over his nose against the stench of disease and death. A close-up revealed an unforgettable image — prisoners had been made to dig their own graves, then shot where they stood. Dead, ravaged bodies with entangled limbs lay where they'd fallen in the mass grave.

The film flickered again. US soldiers were giving the liberated prisoners cigarettes. A group of men sat in a row on a rough wooden bench, each with a cigarette. The cigarettes were lit but dangled between boney fingers. Their haunted eyes made the audience wonder if they truly understood their new circumstances. What did liberation mean to these sufferers? Where were their loved ones? Where would they go? What would they do? There was no one left. Nothing left. Everything was gone.

Liza, Max and Vera couldn't look away. To take their eyes off the despairing images, even for a second, felt as if they were abandoning their loved ones. Filled with panic, they searched the faces of the liberated men, women and children, looking for someone from their past — a family member, a friend, an acquaintance — anyone. Let them be alive.

The film clip ended abruptly and the theatre fell into darkness. Those few minutes of horror had revealed only the smallest fraction of the Nazi's reign of terror.

Liza could not swallow, nor make a sound. Tightness engulfed Max's chest as the reality of what he'd seen sank in. Vera's eyes and mouth were wide open in shock. No one said a word. Then murmurings were heard in the darkness. There were tears muffled behind crumpled hankies, while others whispered prayers. Max felt the kind weight of a hand on his shoulder, but he could not turn around. Time stood still for the three Nafthals, the images of the survivors imprinted forever on their minds.

Suddenly the big screen lit up again, and everyone blinked. The feature film was about to begin. Loud music spilled from the speakers, the sound of popping corn came in from the lobby, and viewers made slurping noises through straws. Just like that, normal life resumed.

But Liza, Max and Vera weren't ready for 'normal.' Without a word, they got up from their seats. As they walked up the aisle, kind hands from their community reached out to them. Silently they reached back as they made their way out the door.

No one knows what words were spoken in the Nafthal home that night, but the next morning the hunt for their family continued. Homes, businesses, money and valuables stolen during the war years were of no importance; only family mattered.

Gradually the shocking reality emerged. Post-war reports disclosed horrific stories, with the estimated numbers of murdered Jews climbing daily — from hundreds, to thousands and soon millions. The world was stunned to learn that so many innocent men, women and children had been murdered. But life had to go on, even at the farm.

On September 28, 1945, twenty-six days after the end of the war, Liza received her official certification as a naturalized Canadian. Liza and Max now had a choice — remain in Nova Scotia or to return and start over in Europe. If they stayed in Canada, their farming commitment to Canadian Immigration would be complete in less than two years. They would then be free to move anywhere in the country. Liza and Max both agreed — they would never return to Europe and had no intentions of ever leaving the farm.

By December 3, 1946, the Naturalization Act was abolished and replaced with the Canadian Citizenship Act. Liza, Max and Vera automatically became full Canadian citizens. The Nafthal family took enormous pride in their adopted country and their new citizenship — but it was a bittersweet moment in the middle of the loss they faced.

The persecution of the Jews was impossible to understand — extreme exclusion, demoralizing humiliation, gruelling labour, horrifying starvation, cruel intimidation, inconceivable brutality and an overwhelming death count. The Nafthals found refuge and lived their lives, but the long struggle with silent survivors' guilt and the enormous loss lay buried deep in their souls — especially Max. "Why did we escape and so many perish?" he often demanded.

Liza and Max's extended families were huge — surely some of them must have survived. Max continued to work with Canadian Immigration, but there was nothing else to be done. The painful wait continued, hoping for a telegram, a letter, or the telephone to ring.

---

After the initial shock at the movie theater, Mom and Nanny were of two minds concerning the newsreels that featured Holocaust survivors. My mother would watch with a fierce intensity, hoping to find someone she knew. My grandmother would turn away, frightened she would find a familiar face. Neither woman ever found anyone.

My family members were arrested for being Jewish. Hitler obliterated them from the human race, and the Nazis robbed them of everything they owned — right down to the hair on their heads and the gold fillings in their teeth. The families were gone, and their possessions too — businesses, homes, paintings, art, stocks and bonds, bank accounts, jewels, vehicles, furniture — everything, large or small.

Survivors told shocking stories during interviews, and as the heinous truths emerged, individual Nazis were hunted down and charged with war crimes. The survivors' stories were confirmed with newsreels, as well as the impeccable documentation and meticulous recordkeeping of the Nazis themselves.

My grandparents and mother got out of bed each day. They moved on with their lives; there was no other choice. Today, however, we know trauma isn't overcome that easily. In one way or another, the pain manifests through generations. My family's secret horrors lived somewhere deep in their emotions — and now and again they would remember. How could they not?

In my younger years, I was frightened by what I didn't know. I knew the Holocaust was horrific, but I didn't know the details, and I never understood how close my grandparents and mother came to a horrifying end. A piece of my life had always been missing — my family's history.

Chapter 47

# Home from War

**In late 1945, the** Allied soldiers returned from war. Joe was not among them — as he had been transferred back to England for the last year of the war. It took him another year to be demobilized out of the service. Joe couldn't wait to return to Vera, but it was very difficult to find passage to North America. Fortunately, Max had shipping connections. He was able to secure passage for Joe on a "Lend-Lease Ship"[99] heading for New York. The ship was an aircraft carrier transporting warplanes that were no longer needed. Just outside New York Harbour, Joe worked with the crew to push the planes off the ship into the ocean. "It was quite a sight!" claimed Joe.

From New York, Joe quickly made his way back to his beautiful wife, and the couple was finally reunited. Everyone could see Vera and Joe adored each other, and it did not take long for their love to produce its first fruit. The Nafthal/Goldston family began to grow. Liza and Max were thrilled — family meant everything.

Most of the men from Greenwood base had already returned home, leaving Liza and Max's large house half empty. The second floor of the farmhouse was equipped with four good-sized bedrooms, a living room, a small kitchen and a bathroom. The rooms circled a grand hall — the perfect gathering place for a growing family. It was also a great space for parties and dancing. Liza and Max gave the newlyweds the upstairs flat, and Vera and Joe immediately made it their home. Now it was time for Joe to prove himself, and Max thought the farm was a perfect place to start.

Although the farm was thriving, Max's heart and soul remained in the lumber business, and so he formed a partnership with Maritime Lumber Distributors, managing the Annapolis Valley operations. Max was thrilled to be back in the timber trade.

In the meantime, recognizing Joe's potential, Max hired his son-in-law to manage the farm under his supervision. This freed up more time for Max to spend with Maritime Lumber Distributors and to research new opportunities in Nova Scotia.

---

Shortly after my father came home from the war, my mother found herself expecting her first child. Within nine years my parents had four children, including me. They were well on their way to fulfilling Mom's dream of a large family.

I can still remember playing in the grand hallway of our upstairs flat. We'd ride our tricycles, pull wagons, and push toy strollers all day long. Marbles would roll, balls of every size and colour would bounce, and toy trucks and trains would plow through dolls, making my sisters and I screech at the top of our lungs. Some evenings my parents would invite all their friends from town to their home for parties. The children's play area was transformed into a party room equipped with loud music and dancing until the wee hours of the morning. There was no insulation between our floor and my grandparents' flat below. What a racket we must have made! Mom told me our grandparents never complained about all the noise — not once, ever. This did not surprise me. I can only imagine how much they must have cherished us, wanting us nearby at any cost — even their peace and quiet. My grandparents continue to amaze me, and my love, appreciation and respect for them have grown ever stronger while writing their story.

My mother and father's marriage remained the greatest love affair I've ever witnessed. It was a rare oddity in the world then, and even today. There is a great deal more to say about Vera and Joe's true love. Perhaps someone else will write their story one day.

Chapter 48

# Out of the Ashes of Hell: Ursula's Story

**Reports of Nazi atrocities** continued to pour out of Europe and across the ocean. Hitler's obsession with cruel, needless killings was impossible for any human being to understand. The final horrifying count echoed all over the world — six million Jews had been murdered during the Holocaust. This did nothing to raise Liza and Max's hope of finding missing family members.

In late 1945, a letter came for Max from the British military base at Neumunster, Germany. News of a relative had finally arrived. Flight Lieutenant Pat Wilson informed the family that he was writing on behalf of Max's niece, Ursula Nafthal. Ursula, known as Ulla, was the middle child of Max's brother Nathan. Ulla had survived the Holocaust and was now living and working on the British military base, where she would stay until she was reunited with her relatives in Canada.[100] The family was overjoyed with the news. Liza and Max had no idea how this miracle had happened.

From that moment on, Max focused on helping his niece. He didn't waste a minute, immediately contacting Canadian Immigration to start the process of bringing Ulla home. What no one realized was just how long the process would take, thanks to government red tape. The only other thing they could do in the meantime was to send Ulla packages filled with clothing, necessities, and treats.

The evening Max received the letter, he went to his desk and pulled out a hardcover ledger. He opened the book with the names of the missing Nafthal and Isserlin family members, then ran down the lists until he came to 'Ursula.' He placed a small checkmark by her name, the only check in the ledger. He continued to turn the pages one at a time, looking over the long lists of missing family, friends, acquaintances, and past employees. Then he went back to the list of family members and stared at the names. It was some time before he closed the book. "One checkmark out of so many," he thought. "But it's a start." Max did not yet realize that this one checkmark would be the last for the Nafthal side of the family.

Meanwhile, in Germany, Ulla anxiously waited for news. More than anything, she wanted to leave and reunite with her family in Canada. Finally, Uncle Max's letter and package arrived. Life was improving for Ulla — at last, she could see a future.

One day, Max received his first letter from Ulla. Before opening the envelope, he thought back to March 22, 1939, the last time he had seen his niece. It was the day he said goodbye to his brother Nathan, his sister-in-law Helene, and their two children, Ulla and Alfred. The family had fled Memel just hours before the Nazis seized the city. Max had offered Nathan his apartment in Kaunas, Lithuania, and Nathan had believed they would be safe there until Hitler's madness was stopped. They never dreamed Hitler would take power over all of Lithuania.

Now Max slipped his letter opener through the envelope, removed the single sheet of paper and Ulla's story began to unfold.

*Dear Uncle Max,*

*I am so glad we are connected and I look forward to our reunion in Canada.*

*Thank you for the letter and package I received today. I could not believe my eyes — soap, shampoo, deodorant, undergarments, and so many treats. The clothes are a little big for me, but I am now fed well, and the clothes will soon make me feel like my old self again.*

*I don't want you to have false hope; I will tell you so you know now. Shortly after we arrived in Kaunas, my mother's cancer progressed quickly. Father sent her to a hospital in Riga, Latvia, where she died in February 1940. We were all very sad that she was alone, but now I see she was one of the lucky ones to die in a warm, comfortable bed.*

*My father, brother, and I were together for a long time, but they lost hope. Both were murdered. I don't know of any other family members. I will tell you more when we are together. I am sorry for the bad news.*

*Love from your niece;*
*Ulla*

Max's tears flowed; what he had suspected was now confirmed as reality. Finally drying his eyes, he again opened his ledger and let his fingers run down a family page until he came to the names Nathan, Helene, and Alfred. He picked up his pen and wrote the words, *died, cancer, Latvia hospital, March 1940* beside his sister-in-law's name. Max stared at the page for a long time, then leaned over and began to write the word *murdered* beside his brother and nephew's names. "How many more will there be?" he wondered. He gave his head a quick shake. Max's main focus had to stay on Ulla — he discovered it wasn't going to be easy to bring her to Canada.

Not grasping the considerable red tape of immigration, Ulla believed she would soon be reunited with her family. Eventually, she received her new Lithuanian passport, but months went by as she waited for her Canadian entrance permit. People came and went from the army base while poor Ulla remained. She made many friends while she continued to work, and soon it was 1946. The packages Ulla received from her uncles Max, Sally and Felix made her more comfortable while she waited for her new life to begin. In addition, Ulla was finally writing to her older sister, Hilde, in Palestine.[101]

But there were harsh realities to battle. As time passed, Ulla began to lose her iron nerve. She became shy as she faced the fierce hatred of many German people. Although difficult to believe, numerous Germans now called the Nazis 'victims of the Jews.' Many Germans refused to believe the horrors of the Holocaust.[102]

Ulla was caught in the middle — the British military on the base loved her, but the Germans despised her. Hardened from the past, Ulla refused to show her deep-seated anguish and intense fear on the surface. That would only give the Germans satisfaction. But deep inside, Ulla longed for her Uncle Max and the safety and comfort of her family.[103]

Chapter 49

# Ulla Reunites with Her Family

**Liza and Max continued** to worry about their niece, Ulla. In January 1947, Ulla was still in Europe waiting for her Canadian immigration papers. She wrote to the family.

*Dear Uncle Max and Aunt Liza;*
*Thank you again and again for all your packages. The items you, Uncle Felix, and Uncle Sally send me make my life a little easier.*

*I smile on the outside for everyone to see. On the inside, however, I am fearful and angry. I want my new life to begin. I want to go to Canada to live with my family and never return to Europe again.*[104]

*Your loving niece,*
*Ulla*

Later in 1947, Ulla finally arrived in Canada. When she first entered the farmhouse, she couldn't believe her eyes. There in the living-room, were the same paintings, accessories and furniture from

Liza and Max's apartment in Memel. She wandered around the room in amazement, looking and touching everything. The same table and buffets stood in the dining-room that she remembered from her childhood! How could this be when she had lost everything?

Liza and Max did not push Ulla to talk about her life during the Holocaust. She wouldn't have talked anyway. She never did, but that didn't stop her from remembering.

After living on the farm for about a week, Ulla rose from her bed in the dark of night. She was always chilled so she wrapped herself tightly in a warm woolen blanket. Ulla picked up the notebook and pen that Aunt Liza had left in her room. With the blanket dragging behind her on the wooden floors, Ulla wandered out of her bedroom and into the dimness of the house. She stopped at her uncle's hat table, placed a finger near the centre of the glass top and twirled it around on its axle. As she watched it move round and round, she remembered her own father's hat table so similar to this one — an item she hadn't thought of in many years. Tears welled up in her eyes as so many memories returned. Mere things but such a reminder of her own losses — family, friends and everything they knew and owned. She wandered into the living-room and curled her legs under her in Aunt Liza's oversized chenille chair. It was the same chair she'd sat in many times during her other life, the one before the Holocaust. Aside from the nighttime creaks of the large house, the room was an eerie silence.

Ulla finally allowed her mind to drift back to the beginning. She clicked on the floor lamp, opened the notebook to the blank first page and began to write.

*There were three of us, my father, my brother Alf and me living in Uncle Max's apartment in Kaunas. All went well until July 15, 1940. The Russians were still allies of the Germans and they arrived and occupied the city.*

*The Russian authorities confiscated all my father's businesses and assets. He could no longer work, but I did and we lived.*

*Life continued until Hitler invaded Kaunas on July 22, 1941. I turned on the radio, "Heil! Heil! Heil Hitler!"*

*The Nazis had taken possession of Kaunas. That evening horses, troops and guns were in terrific numbers everywhere. The shops closed so there was no more access to food — or anything else.*

*Brutal violence began.*

*I witnessed killings on the streets. Round-ups occurred often, but I saved myself from many close calls with my new-found cheekiness, courage, fair complexion and fluent German.*

*Within a week, I was fired from my job because I was a Jew; no other reason. I was lucky to walk away with my life.*

*On the very same day, the Nazis confiscated the family's apartment. All Jewish people faced the same problems, or even worse. No money, no food, and no home; many lost their will to live. We stayed with a neighbour for a short time.*

*Nazis enforced the order that all Jews must wear a yellow star — if you were caught without a star you were shot. Either way, we were moving targets. The Germans gave orders for all Jews to relocate to the ghetto. There was no choice.*

*Whether young, old, or sick, all Jews received work orders.*

*Soon the Nazis enclosed the ghetto with a heavily barbed-wire fence. The guards were ordered to shoot to kill anyone who tried to leave without authorization — and they did.*

*The overcrowding, filth and danger in the ghetto were appalling. To protect my family when there were round-ups, I made a hiding place under the floorboards —which worked. Father, Alf and I were sick, feverish and hungry but we continued. My courage never deserted me.*

*Every day there was less food than the day before. People were starving to death. Many dead in the streets.*

*Working conditions worsened due to the captives lack of strength, inadequate food and clothing, bad weather, and disease.*

*Then it happened to us in May 1944, Alf was the first to be taken and the parting nearly tore out my heart!*

Tears rolled down Ulla's cheeks as she thought about her younger brother. If only he could have been saved, he'd be here with her now. Life would be so much better with Alf. But that was not reality, and Ulla was a realist.

*Soon the remaining captives were forced out of the ghetto. Father and I were marched to the harbour where there was a waiting cargo ship. We walked on the single plank that led into the dark belly of the boat where we sat exhausted. We asked for water — but there was none. One day passed, then eight days with little food and water. We finally landed — we left Lithuania behind.*

*We were marched straight into a large hall at the Stutthof Concentration Camp — a place spoken of with terror. The men were taken away including father. I never saw him again.*

*S.S. women circulated among us with orders and worse. I was alive but I saw myself as a corpse.*

*The daily routine of the concentration camp started — it was grueling. We were hot, filthy, hungry, thirsty, tired, nervous and sick — yet we fought each day for a bit of rotting food, and a place at the overcrowded tap for water.*

Ulla wondered now how she had ever kept her chin up, even managing to laugh now and then. Perhaps this was the secret of her survival.

*Soon we were working —hard labour — if you fell, you were left behind.*

*Disease flourished — so many people died. There was no medication to treat any illnesses and I was often sick. I still wanted to live and be cheerful — so I was.*

*September 1,1945 the Holocaust ended. I was not among the overwhelming death count, but my living Hell didn't end there. Still, I lived — and here I am.*[105]

Ulla suddenly realized dawn had arrived. She watched the golden sun come up over the horizon and heard creaking floors, a door opening and water running. Soon, Aunt Liza appeared in the living room — and stopped short when she saw Ulla curled up in a blanket staring out the window. Liza wondered about all the terrors that plagued her niece, her eyes filled as she thought for the hundredth time, there was nothing she could do. Ulla turned her head towards Liza and their sad eyes met, both wondering if the other would ever understand. Liza was well aware that she had escaped a living Hell, while Ulla knew she could never explain the Holocaust terrors that still haunted her.

Suddenly the back kitchen door opened and the housekeeper called out her usual 'good morning'. Liza and Ulla shook their heads and wiped their eyes. The spell of grief, loss and horror was broken as another day began. Ulla tucked the notebook into a hiding place and didn't write again for many years.

By New Year's of 1948, after seven months on the farm, Ulla had enough. After eight years of Holocaust Hell, Ulla moved to Halifax and started a new chapter in her life.[106]

---

Ulla's father Nathan had held power of attorney for all of Max's assets in Memel and Lithuania, meaning that when the Soviet Union confiscated all of Nathan's wealth, they also seized Max's properties. At the end of WWII, Russian authorities refused to provide compensation for all they had stolen from innocent Jews. Max and Nathan's wealth in Europe was gone without a trace. But Max let that go, he only cared about bringing Ulla to Canada and finding other family members.

Ulla eventually married Ernest Freedman, moved to Montreal and had two sons, Norman (Norm) and Mark. The couple also had a daughter who died when she was three months old. Yet another great loss in Ulla's life.

According to Ulla's eldest son Norman his mother never talked about her experiences in the Holocaust — not to her children nor to her Nova Scotia relatives. Ulla was of the same mind as Liza and Vera — she rarely talked about the horrors of the Holocaust years. Yet sometimes, for no apparent reason she would give her sons a glimpse into the past. What Ulla did do was write her detailed memoirs and gave a copy to each son when she felt they were old enough to understand.

Ulla's husband, Ernest, wanted to publish Ulla's memoirs shortly after they were written, but she refused. Ulla was paranoid about her information being misused by the Germans. Norm feels that Ulla has been gone a long time and that her story needs to be shared. I agree, and with Norm's permission, my next great writing adventure is Ulla's story.

Chapter 50

# Max M. Nafthal Ltd.

> Around 1945/46, Vati started the pit prop business. This was the first time that pit prop had been produced here in Nova Scotia, where until this time pulpwood and logging had been the major industries. In 1951 my father incorporated his company as Max M. Nafthal Ltd. The company employed 300-600 people, depending on the season, in its forestry, milling and farming operations throughout Western Nova Scotia and beyond.
>
> My father missed here all the dark rye bread he was used to at home, and my mother learned to bake this for him. In those days it was 'make your own' or import, and his love for good food made him expend considerable energy to obtain his favourites.
>
> -VERA OLGA (NAFTHAL) GOLDSTON

**Max continued to work** in partnership with the Maritime Lumber Distributors, managing operations in the Annapolis Valley. In 1945, Max signed a contract with the British Ministry of War Transport to provide discharge ballast for their ships. Discharge ballast refers to the logs on a vessel that increases draft, changes the trim, regulate stability or maintain stress loads.

The contract gave Max the confidence to branch out, and once again he formed his own lumber company. In 1951, Max incorporated his company as Max M. Nafthal Ltd. While Europeans did not have a middle name, Max loved the Canadian custom of using a second name or initial and adopted his Hebrew name, Meyer, as his middle name. He took great pride every time he signed his name — Max M. Nafthal. For the first time in his life, Max used his Hebrew name for business.

Over the next few years, Max developed a pit prop business in the Annapolis Valley — the first production venture of its kind in Nova Scotia. Pit props are peeled, five-foot logs, used to secure the roofs in coal mine tunnels.

There was a huge demand for pit prop in the United States and Britain. In the 1950s, Max opened offices all over Nova Scotia, with the main office in Middleton, and satellite offices in Digby, Shelburne, Yarmouth, Port Williams and Bridgewater. Max continued to build the business by purchasing woodlands throughout the province and creating lumber camps producing pit prop. Business boomed. Twenty to thirty ships were loaded with pit prop annually in the tiny port town of Digby. As a result, the sleepy town received a tremendous economic boost, about $10,000 with each ship (equivalent to $116,658.92 in 2022). This was a small fortune in the 1950s. Ships generated economic activity in multiple ways; from boat maintenance and parts to food and supplies, entertainment, meals and accommodations for crew members on leave.

Max became even more active in the lumber business, purchasing lumber from all over Nova Scotia, including Cape Breton, and shipping it to the United States and Europe. Lumber was shipped from the ports of Digby, Yarmouth, Port Williams, Bridgewater and Halifax. To get the lumber to these harbours, ground transportation was required — so Max created a large trucking fleet that operated throughout the province. At a time when Nova Scotia had limited employment opportunities, Max's offices, lumber camps and fleet of trucks provided employment for many Nova Scotians.

It was astonishing that Max was able to divide his time between the farm and the booming lumber business. Max's son-in-law, Joe, continued to co-manage the farm with Max. As Max's business grew, there were more opportunities for Joe.

Joe was also employed as the bookkeeper for Max M. Nafthal Ltd. By 1954, Joe had obtained his Provincial Scaler's License. As a log scaler, he measured cut trees to determine the volume and grade of the wood to be used for manufacturing. Joe had proven himself on the farm and in the lumber business. Working and living with his father-in-law was not always easy, but Joe took it in stride. He appreciated the opportunities and enjoyed the times when Max was away travelling for business.

Max M. Nafthal Ltd. quickly grew into the largest shipper of pulpwood and pit prop in Nova Scotia. The company employed between 300–600 workers, depending on the season. The business was thriving in the offices, in the camps and on the farm. But Max was a man who never forgot anyone, and during the winter months, he would purchase pit props from the local farmers — as long as they hauled the logs to the roadside. He would send Joe out to scale the pit props, and then send a truck to pick them up. Since there was no employment insurance or farmers' government assistance this was a great source of income for small farmers who often suffered financially in the cold months.

The farm continued to expand. In the early 1950s, Canada had an excess of apple growers, and so the government offered a grant to farmers to cut down their apple orchards and transition to a new crop. Max cut down his apple orchards and planted the first successful alfalfa crops in the region.

Max's achievements paid off. He helped Nova Scotia's depressed economy by providing significant employment opportunities. Max M. Nafthal Ltd. was known throughout Nova Scotia and beyond. The farm became the focal point of many social and professional gatherings, and everyone loved the meals prepared in Liza's kitchen. Max took great pride in their growing family, his lumber business, their prosperous farm and their stately home. The good life was back.

---

Grampy claimed that of all the timber merchants he apprenticed with, he was the only one to survive the Holocaust. He must have gone to great lengths and spent much time and money looking for his friends and family. How else would he have known this?

My grandfather often spent time working in Digby — always staying at the same small hotel. Food was still very important to him, but the meals found in Digby were too plain for his European palette. The only exception was the Hedley House. Nanny and Mom often drove up to visit — always bringing him a basket of home-cooking. Grampy loved to see Nanny's home-baked European dark rye bread in the picnic boxes she packed.

The ships Grampy did business with often invited him for meals, and he especially enjoyed the familiar European cuisine offered on Scandinavian, Dutch and French vessels. On his frequent business trips to Montreal and New York, he spent a considerable amount of energy tracking down those favourite European foods that were unavailable in Nova Scotia. Grampy always returned from these trips with a large kosher salami under his arm. Mom claimed her father was "a personal importer of European foods."

---

I remember how devastated I was when the farmhands cut down the apple orchards. One of the orchards faced my bedroom windows — as the seasons changed, I saw bare branches in winter and the green leaves of spring. Later there were beautiful pink and white blossoms, then a September crop of bright red apples. But what I missed most was running and playing among the trees. I still remember running through the orchard with my sister and brother. I remember the smell of the new wooden apple barrels. And, I remember seeing pickers climbing into the well-laden branches of the trees using wooden ladders to reach the top. The trucks moved in and out of the orchid, leaving with their red-cheeked fruit — only to return later for their next great load. My connection to the alfalfa crops could never match what I'd felt for the old apple orchards.

Yes, to this day I miss the apple orchards of my childhood.

Chapter 51

# Murdered

> After the Holocaust they had disappeared, and nothing could ever be traced about them, just vanished, together with six million other Jews. Everything for Jews ended in a pyre.
>
> -VERA OLGA (NAFTHAL) GOLDSTON

A LIST OF HOLOCAUST victims is available for the public to view in the Central Database of Shoah Victims' Names at the Yad Vashem, World Holocaust Remembrance Centre in Israel. Shoah, which means "catastrophe" in Hebrew, is the Jewish name for the Holocaust. In 1967, when Liza visited Israel, there were no names to be found for the Isserlin and Nafthal family members, however, there is more information in this database today.

## The Isserlins

**Mania Isserlin Sheyniuk**

- age 47, murdered in 1941, Vilna Ghetto, Vilnius, Lithuania

**Kolia Sheyniuk**

- age unknown, murdered in 1941, Vilna Ghetto, Vilnius, Lithuania

**Olga Sheyniuk**

- age 19, murdered in 1941, Vilna Ghetto, Vilnius, Lithuania

Mania Isserlin Sheyniuk was Liza's older sister. During the war, Mania and her family resided in Wilna, Poland. She was born in Moscow on April 20, 1894, and was listed as a housewife. Kolia Sheyniuk is Mania's husband and was listed as a businessman; his birthdate is unknown. Their daughter Olga was born in 1922. She was listed as a child and student.

**Grisha Isserlin**

- age 36, murdered in 1941, Vilna Ghetto, Vilnius, Lithuania

**Ariela Isserlin**

- age unknown, murdered in 1941, Vilna Ghetto, Vilnius, Lithuania

Grisha was Liza's younger brother, born in Moscow in 1905. Before WWII, Grisha was listed as a merchant. He was living with his wife Ariela in Warsaw, Poland. It is not known if the couple had children.

Ghettos isolated Jews from the non-Jewish population and other Jewish communities. Living conditions were both brutal and deadly. Vilna Ghetto in Vilnius, Lithuania, existed for approximately two years. Life in the ghetto meant starvation, disease, beatings, maltreatment and executions on the streets. Most Jews imprisoned in the ghetto also faced deportation to concentration and extermination camps. For these reasons, an estimated initial population of 40,000 in Vilna Ghetto ultimately decreased to zero. Several hundred people did manage to survive by hiding in the forests surrounding the city, sheltering with sympathetic locals, or joining Soviet partisans. The partisans made significant contributions to the war by frustrating German plans to economically exploit occupied Soviet territories. They conducted systematic strikes against Germany's communication network and interfered with political work among the local population.[107]

# The Nafthals

### Alfred (Alf) Nafthal

- age unknown, murdered in 1944, Kovno Ghetto

Alfred was Nathan's youngest child and only son — making him Liza and Max's nephew. He did survive for some time at Kovno Ghetto, however, he was eventually taken away and never seen by his father and sister, Ursula again.

The Kovno Ghetto was established by Nazi Germany as a forced labour camp to hold the Lithuanian Jews of Kaunas during the Holocaust. Later German, Austrian and Czech Jews were shipped to Kovno. The ghetto was extremely overcrowded, with little food and no sewer system which caused epidemics such as typhus. Most imprisoned Jews were later sent to concentration and extermination camps, or shot at the Ninth Fort. Ninth Fort was a killing site four miles away, which served as a place of torture and mass executions for Jewish men, women and children in Kovno Ghetto. Few survived.[108]

### Nathan Nafthal

- age 56, murdered in 1945, Dachau Concentration Camp, Bavaria, Germany

Nathan was Max's brother, born in Memel in 1889. He was predeceased by his wife, Helene, who had died of cancer in the early days of the war. Helene passed away in a hospital in Riga, Latvia, without family or friends. Ulla and Nathan survived the horrors of Kovno Ghetto.

Dachau was the first Nazi concentration camp constructed in Germany. It opened, in 1933, and originally held political prisoners. It eventually became a death camp and the site of cruel medical experiments. Thousands of Jews suffered and died of disease, malnutrition and overwork, while others were executed.[109]

### Hanna Nafthal Wolfsohn

- age 53, murdered in 1944, Stutthof Concentration Camp, Germany

### David Wolfsohn

- age unknown, murdered in 1944, Stutthof Concentration Camp, Germany

Hanna was Max's only sister. She was born in 1891 in Memel, Lithuania, and was listed as having no profession. David Wolfsohn was her husband; his birthdate and profession are unknown. The couple lived in Kaunas, Lithuania, during the war. It is not known whether they had children.

Stutthof Concentration Camp was located in a marshy, wooded area of Stutthof, Germany. The prisoners who were too weak for forced labour were sent to the gas chambers. Conditions were severe, and many died from a typhus epidemic. The camp's prisoners were subject to cruelty, forced evacuation, lack of medical care, and murder.[110]

**Bernard Nafthal**

- age unknown, murdered in Riga Ghetto, Latvia

**Ditta Nafthal**

- age 11 years old, murdered in Riga Ghetto, Latvia

Bernard was Max's brother, born in 1893 in Memel, Lithuania. The name and fate of his wife are unknown. Ditta was his daughter.

In September 1941, German Jews were deported to east Germany. As a result of overcrowding, the trains were rerouted to the Riga Ghetto, Latvia. Bernard and his family had been living in Hanover, Germany, and were likely relocated to Riga around this time. Residents of Riga faced overcrowding, poor sanitation, contaminated drinking water and mass killings.[111]

---

With the exception of Ulla's news, the family claimed they didn't have details of what happened during the Holocaust. Liza and Max only knew that their family members didn't reappear after the war. Liza, Max and Vera were left to assume they'd been murdered — without knowing where or when.

Today the internet is a wonderful source of history. To date, I have found the family members listed above, with the place and year of their deaths. The cause of death in each case was listed as 'murdered.' The large Isserlin and Nafthal families included many other grandparents, aunts, uncles and cousins, spanning decades. I don't have the names of the others, so my focus still remains on Liza and Max's immediate family. I almost gave up hope of finding another family member — and then, I found Joesph Cukierman and his family.

Alexander (Alex) is from my grandmother's side of the family — the Isserlins. His parents were Julia and Joseph Cukierman which makes Alex — Liza's first cousin once removed. As Alex's story began to unfold, it took me back to the desperate telegrams my grandparents received requesting help to flee Europe. I couldn't help but wonder if one of those telegrams came from Alex's parents.

Joseph Cukierman was a Polish born doctor and world champion chess player. In the late 1920's, both Joseph and Julia Cukierman were living in Paris, France — where they met and married sometime in, 1933. In 1938, the couple's only child, Alex, was born.

The Cukiermans found themselves trapped in Europe at the beginning of the war. When Germany invaded France, Joseph's fame as a chess player threatened to bring dangerous Nazi attention to his family. In 1940, they fled Paris with the intention of reaching Spain, however, they got stuck in Castres, east of Toulouse in southern

France. Joseph died later that same year — and Julia told Alex the Nazis had murdered his father.

Following Joseph's death, Julia and Alex moved to Vabres, a small mountain village fifty kilometres from Castres, where they hid in plain sight among the village's Catholic and Huguenot[112] population. When the village priest warned Julia that the French militia was looking for her, she and Alex hid in a monastery for six months. During 1947, they emigrated to Palestine to reunite with Julia's family.

When Alex was sixteen-years-old, he returned to Paris where he met a family from his father's village in Poland. They implied that Joseph committed suicide by jumping off a roof. No one believed he'd been suicidal, and yet, they knew Joseph dreaded the coming fate of the European Jews.

Over the years, Alex collected conflicting accounts of his father's death. His mother's half-sister, Eva, told him that Joseph was being tracked by the French militia who were cooperating with the Nazis. She believed that in his depressed state, Joseph was convinced his death would keep his young wife and son safe.

Alexander Alekhine, an adversary champion chess player offered a quote found in an archived newspaper article from, 1941, "Joseph threw himself from a balcony for no apparent reason, since he enjoyed excellent health and fortune."[113]

Alex considered these accounts and couldn't help but find a parallel between his father's death and Kristallnacht, the night of the broken glass. During the Kristallnacht many heinous crimes were committed against the Jewish population including — pushing Jews out of upstairs windows and roofs to their deaths below. Alex also wondered why a doctor would jump to his death when he had access to any number of drugs.

Eighty years later, Alex is still haunted by this mystery. He is about seventy-five percent convinced that his father's death was the unpremeditated suicide of a desperate man trying to protect his wife and son. Alex is about twenty-five percent convinced the French militia staged his father's death to look like a suicide.[114]

In 1966, my grandmother travelled to Israel to visit Julia's half-sister, Eva and her family. Nanny was also looking for information at the Yad Vashem Holocaust Museum[115] — in particular her sister Mania and brother Grisha. She was unsuccessful in her search. Julia had passed away several years before my grandmother's visit. I don't know if Liza and Julia ever reconnected after the war. I assume there were letters.

During 1977 or 1978, Alex visited my grandmother in Canada with his first wife, Nurit, and their two oldest children, Tali and Dani. Although the visit was pleasant, it was the only time he met Liza.

I am honoured to include a brief account of Julia and Joseph's story. My hope is that other children of Holocaust survivors — or the first generation born afterward — will find the courage to share their stories before they are lost forever.

Chapter 52

# Max M. Nafthal: Two Funerals

> On December 26, 1957, my father died very suddenly of a heart attack following an appendectomy.
>
> —VERA OLGA (NAFTHAL) GOLDSTON

**Sometime in the early** 1950s, Max went to the funeral of a business associate. He was surprised he did not recognize anyone at the event; however, he was quite taken with the beautiful floral arrangements in every corner of the church. The service also had enough humour to make it enjoyable. Early in the sermon, he realized he was attending the wrong funeral. Max loved people and food, so he stayed afterward for the reception. He was so impressed with this event, he reported every tiny detail to Liza, including the impressive turnout and his conversations with several guests. Max loved a good funeral.

While at home in mid-December 1957, Max experienced excruciating pain. He was rushed by ambulance to Blanchard-Fraser Memorial Hospital in Kentville, where he was diagnosed with appendicitis and underwent emergency surgery. Following his surgery, Max rested in the hospital for a week. He was looking forward to coming home and convalescing under Liza's care, and so, fully dressed, sitting on the edge of the bed, he waited for his wife to pick him up.

Liza was about to leave for the hospital when the telephone rang. She rushed to answer, listened, then slowly lowered the receiver. Her tears flowed quickly, followed by sobs. She tried to pull herself together, but it was impossible. She needed Vera who was upstairs in her flat. Liza rushed into the hallway and opened the door to the apartment.

I remember that day. I was six years old, sitting at the top of the stairs, playing with my dolls. When Nanny looked up, we caught each other's eyes. It was the first time I'd seen my grandmother cry. Tears poured down her face as she cried out, "Where is your mother?" Without a word I jumped up, forgetting my dolls as I ran to find Mom. I told her Nanny was crying, and my mother rushed to the stairs. I chased after Mom, not wanting to leave her side. We met Nanny on the landing.

"What's happened, Mutti?" Mom's voice was filled with fear.

"Your father is dead!"

I clung to my mother's leg. Mom cried out as she grabbed hold of Nanny. I cried out too because the two women I depended on most were frightening me. Hearing the commotion, our housekeeper, Elsie, rushed in to take me away. I don't remember anything more about that day, or the days that followed.

This is what actually happened.

On December 26, 1957, Max was fully dressed and sitting on the side of his hospital bed waiting for Liza to pick him up. He suddenly went into cardiac arrest, fell backward and died instantly. Max M. Nafthal was 61 years old. The pain of his loss was unbearable, but despite the agony, Liza had to take control once again.

Liza knew Max would want a traditional Jewish funeral, and she planned to give him one. This task was not as easy as one might think. The rabbi at the Baron de Hirsch Synagogue in Halifax refused to perform the ceremony unless the family agreed to bury Max on consecrated land. This meant that Max had to be buried in the Jewish cemetery[116] in Halifax, 96 miles (154 km) away. Liza refused — the site was too far from his family and his farm. Both Liza and the rabbi stood their ground.

Finally, it was decided that Max would be buried on the family farm. A large piece of land bordering the Nictaux Cemetery was chosen, and the Chevra Kadisha[117] was hired to bless and certify the land before Max was buried. Countless other preparations were made and a date for Max's funeral was set.

---

I remember the day of Grampy's funeral. I was standing at my bedroom window, which overlooked our gardens. Beyond the gardens, my grandfather's huge field border the Nictaux Cemetery. Along the length of the cemetery, I could see crowds of people — many dressed in black. Beautiful flowers were piled high everywhere. Cars were parked in the field and close to the cemetery's fence. I had never seen cars in my grandfather's field. Vehicles lined up on both sides of the road to the farm and filled our driveway. Our housekeeper, Elsie, came in to call me away from the window. When I asked her what was happening, she told me people were gathering for Grampy's funeral. I wanted to know why I wasn't invited, and why she wasn't there too. Elsie said she needed to be at home, taking care of me and my brother and sister because we were too young to attend. She told me her husband, Nelson, was there for all of us. I didn't understand the true meaning of a funeral — but I still felt left out.

If only Grampy could have seen the huge gathering of people and beautiful flowers piled everywhere. He would have loved it. After the graveside service, the guests were invited to the farm. A team of caterers stood ready with refreshments, including many of Grampy's favourites. I could hear the commotion below but I was not allowed downstairs. To date, my grandfather's funeral remains the last traditional Jewish funeral in the Nafthal/Goldston family.

Max was survived by his wife Elizabeth (Liza); daughter Vera Olga Nafthal Goldston; son-in-law Joseph Goldston; four young grandchildren — Janet, Jack, Sharon (Sharry), and Peggy; brothers Sally and Felix; sister-in-law Lottie; nieces Hilde, Ursula, grand nieces Tamy, Ilana, and Nadja and grand nephews, Axel, Norman and Mark. In May 1959, Vera gave birth to Max's fifth grandchild, who carries his grandfather's name — Max William (Bill). Except for his niece Ursula, Max was predeceased by all members of both the Nafthal family and the Isserlin family who died in Europe during the Holocaust.

Max's death not only devastated his family and friends but shocked the whole community. Max left behind hundreds of people who had benefited from his business, Max M. Nafthal Ltd. Grief-stricken colleagues, associates, friends and family all felt a great loss.

*"May his memory be a blessing"*

Chapter 53

# Mother and Daughter's Memories

> I was only five or six years old when my Opapa died and I watched the funeral procession from our window. Your great-grandfather was buried beside his wife in the Jewish cemetery in Memel, and this was all ploughed under and destroyed by the Nazis. So much for that.
>
> -VERA OLGA (NAFTHAL) GOLDSTON

In the few pages Mom wrote before her death, she mentioned a time long before the war. Mom was seven years old, a year older than me was when my grandfather — her father — died. In 1932, my mother also stood at a window, watching a parade of mourners walk past for the funeral of Wolfe Nafthal, Mom's beloved grandfather. Just like me! Mom and I never knew we shared a similar experience surrounding our grandfathers' deaths. How sad it is that we didn't share these memories together.

---

Days after my grandfather's funeral, Nanny took me to town to run a few errands. I don't remember being in town, but I do recall we didn't return straight home. Without saying a word, Nanny turned her car into the field bordering the cemetery where my grandfather had been buried the week before. Deep tire impressions led to my grandfather's grave, which was blanketed in a pile of freshly turned soil and covered with bouquets of wilting flowers. Nanny told me to stay in the car. I wanted to chase after her as she opened her door and got out, but I was too afraid. Nanny walked straight over to the dark mound and knelt. For the second time in my life, I watched helplessly as my grandmother cried. I could feel the lump in my throat growing larger; I thought I would burst. I'm not sure how long I sat in the car before Nanny wiped her tears and returned. She drove us home in silence. The lump in my throat was so large, that I wouldn't have been able to talk anyway. The moment she pulled up to the house, I jumped out of the vehicle without saying goodbye. I sprinted across the driveway, ran up to the door, hurried up the stairs, and raced to my bedroom, where I threw myself across my bed and let my tears flow. Mom heard me sobbing, and asked what had happened. I refused to say a word. Dad came in next and asked if I was sick, or if something had happened in town? I just shook my head and continued to cry. I never told my parents about the stop Nanny had made on the way home that day.

While I watched my grandmother at the graveside, I suddenly realized the meaning of death. My grandfather was gone, buried under that mound of dirt. It was an extremely painful experience for such a young child to bear alone. I don't know why I didn't talk to my parents that day. I don't know whether they asked my grandmother if anything happened. It was never talked about again.

Nor did Mom ever talk about Grampy after his death. After all, you don't talk or think about the deceased once they're gone. That life was over.

I can't explain fully, but life was never the same after my grandfather's death. My grief was cut short in childhood, although I carried it within my heart. While I have limited memories of childhood — I have never forgotten that day. Decades have gone by, and I still miss Grampy. While writing this book I had the opportunity to gather loving memories of my grandfather.

---

## Memories of Grampy

Grampy loved a great cigar! Whenever I smell a quality cigar, I still think of Grampy. Not that long ago, I noticed on Facebook that my sister Janet answered the question, "What smell reminds you of something in the past?" Her reply; "Cigar smoke reminds me of my grandfather." I didn't know my sister and I shared the same memory until that day.

Cigars weren't Grampy's only indulgence. He also kept a stash of pink marzipan pigs in his large walk-in closet/dressing-room. Sometimes he'd break off a little piece for me. I thought it was quite normal to have marzipan pigs in one's dressing-room until years later, when I was surprised to learn that it was not! I had no idea why he kept the pigs in his dressing-room until my sister Janet told me the story decades later. She said Grampy wasn't supposed to eat sweets, and so he always hid a stash from Nanny!

He also had an automatic shoe buffer in his dressing-room. I loved to turn it on and stick my bare feet underneath to polish my toes. Between the treats, the shoe buffer, and my grandfather's love for his grandchildren, I wonder now if Grampy ever had a private moment in his dressing-room.

---

One day Grampy had driven himself to Bridgewater, 53 miles,(85 kms) away from his home in Nictaux. Somehow, he managed to drive his brand-new Chrysler into the LaHave River. Fortunately, he wasn't hurt. In my grandfather's style, he just picked up the telephone, called Dad, and told him to go pick up another new Chrysler and bring it to him in Bridgewater.[118]

---

Early in the 1950s, Grampy started a tradition he loved. Towards the end of the year, he gave out hundreds of Max M. Nafthal Ltd. calendars to employees, businesses, farmers, friends and acquaintances. The calendars came rolled in individual cardboard tubes — with about twenty-four to a box — which took up a good deal of space in the office. Grampy always made a great fuss getting the calendars labeled with names and addresses. Then stamps were added before delivering the packages to the post office. This put the office in an uproar for a week. One year when Grampy was away on a business trip, my father got the bright idea to get the calendars out early. Max always got a bit crazy about the calendars — this way the office would stay calm. After all, what could go wrong?

Dad and Tony Pettersen, an accounting clerk and family friend, organized the calendar mail-out. It went smoothly, and Dad and Tony were pleased with themselves. When Max returned to the office, his first question was, "Where are the calendars? We have to get them in the mail before the New Year!"

"Don't worry, Max!" Dad said proudly. "We sent them all out while you were away."

Grampy was flabbergasted and started shouting at the top of his lungs. "What about the girly calendars? Who looked after them?"

"What girly calendars?" said my dad.

So that's when Dad learned, Grampy always ordered a small batch of calendars for some special friends — calendars you wouldn't hang up in your home. But you might spot them in barns and garages around Nova Scotia, out of sight of wives, girlfriends and children. Grampy was sure there would be serious repercussions from the unauthorized mail-out because the Annapolis Valley was largely a Baptist community. To everyone's surprise, they never heard a word. Dad often wondered about the astonished expressions that must have appeared on the faces of those people who received the 'girly calendars.' Grampy was never a boring man![119]

---

Tamy Sturmann was Hilde's daughter. Her grandfather was Nathan Nafthal, making her Max's great-niece. In 1954, twelve-year-old Tamy Sturmann was living in Israel with her parents, Hilde and Hans. That summer, Hilde and Tamy visited the farm in Nictaux. The Nafthals were thrilled to be reunited with Hilde and to meet their grand-niece, Tamy. The visitors were supposed to stay six weeks, but they were so happy and comfortable on the farm that they stayed three months. Unable to come on the visit, Tamy's father, Hans, was in despair back home in Israel.

Tamy said her Great-Uncle Max was extremely generous. Once when Max, Hilde and Tamy were in town, he said, "I'll buy you anything you wish."

"A bicycle!" said Tamy.

"OK," Max said, heading to the store.

Hilde was horrified. "How do I take a bike back to Israel?" Not so easy in 1954!

So instead, Great-Uncle Max gave Tamy money to purchase a bike when she returned home — a dream come true. Tamy has never forgotten that this act of kindness made her the happiest girl on earth — until today she still loves cycling. Tamy and her husband Yoram Rosenbaum have cycled in Holland, Denmark, Finland, south England and Australia.

My grandfather had always been generous. Five years earlier in 1949, he gave Hilde money to purchase a piano, which she played until the age of 97. Hilde died on July 4, 2018, at the age of 104 years old. I am so sorry I never went to Israel to visit her.

Tamy told me her mother, Hilde, loved my family dearly. I was too young to remember their visit in 1954, but she recently sent me a photograph of the three of us — Hilde, Tamy and me — at the beach. We looked so happy together. The photograph of the past, Tamy's fond memories and her loving words are a beautiful gift to me. [120]

---

Dianne Hankinson LeGard also remembers Max fondly. As a child, she spent a significant amount of time on the family farm with her parents, Tom and Peg Hankinson. In the fall of 1956, Dianne was working as a teller in the main branch of the Bank of Nova Scotia in Montreal. Several times a year, Max took the train to Montreal for business. One day around noon, Dianne looked up to see Max standing at the wicket with another gentleman. When Max invited Dianne to lunch, she told him that her lunch break was not until one o'clock. As it happened, the gentleman with Max was the bank manager. He told Dianne it was OK for her to take her break early. Dianne was taken out to lunch at a very upscale restaurant. She laughed as she told me, "Only your grandfather could arrange a lunch like that!" In those days, bank managers did not go out for lunch with tellers. When Dianne got back to the bank, the other tellers wanted to know who Max was, and why she was invited to such a lunch.[121]

I love Dianne's story. It shows Grampy's charisma, and how much he loved everyone. And in turn, everyone loved being around him.

People still remember my grandfather to this day. He had many different titles — son, brother, husband, father, grandfather, uncle, great-uncle, friend, employer and boss. He was a man that people felt safe with — and came to when in need. Grampy quietly supported many people during their hard times, but what made him extra special was that he never talked or boasted about his generosity.

Grampy was loved and mourned from Nova Scotia to Montreal, New York, Europe and Israel. Decades later, he is still missed.

Chapter 54

# Changes

**After Max's death, Liza** had to make some decisions. Max had left no plans for the farm, his lumber business, or his various parcels of land. Max always had a clear vision for all his business ventures — but he kept these plans close to his chest — only sharing them with one man — Jim Christie. Jim, who lived in Bridgewater and worked from the Bridgewater office, was Max's right-hand man. When Max died, Jim was the only person with enough knowledge about the European contracts, shipping companies and inventories, etc. to keep the business going. This made Jim a logical buyer. Liza sold Max M. Nafthal Ltd. to Jim Christie, and in return, Jim gave Liza a good and fair price. Jim moved the head office to Bridgewater, and the office in Middleton was closed.

The sale and business move did not affect Vera's husband, Joe. Finding it difficult to work for his father-in-law and live in the same house, Joe had already moved on. At the time of Max's death, Joe had been out of the family business for a few years. He had fifty percent ownership of A.W. Allen & Son Ltd., a lumber business in Middleton.

Even before Max passed away, Vera and Joe had already talked about moving into town. The children would grow up with more independence: walking to school, visiting friends or the library, playing sports and attending social events. So, Liza made another decision — she sold the farm to a Dutch company called Bonda Farms.

In 1958, the family moved to Middleton. They purchased a piece of property and built two homes side-by-side, with a large, shared driveway between them. Liza lived in one house, and Vera, Joe and the children lived in the other. Liza and Vera continued to live side-by-side until they sold their homes and moved to Halifax in, 1978.

---

I have no idea how my grandmother felt about leaving her beautiful home. My parents had good reasons for their determination to move into town. I'm certain Nanny had no interest in operating the farm on her own, nor would she want to live in such a large house alone.

I was seven years old when we left the farm. My only memory of moving day was running from room to room, kissing every single wall goodbye. I had no idea how much I would miss our life on the farm, or what an empty void my grandfather's death would always leave.

Nanny's home was an oasis. Usually, I was alone with my grandmother — and I loved that. Her door was always unlocked, and she always had time for us. Now that I think back, I'm amazed at how available Nanny was to our family. She had a way of making me believe we were the most important people in her life. There are so many people in this world who have never had the experience and security of being loved and cared for so dearly.

Chapter 55

# The Lost Uncles: Felix and Sally

> Sally became Public Prosecutor in Lithuania until the Germans took the Memelland, when he was of course fired as a Jew. Incidentally, after the war he received annual compensation from the German government for the loss of his job. Also, I believe his work in the law courts helped prevent periodic harassment by the police, and periodic jailing as Jews for our family.
>
> —VERA OLGA (NAFTHAL) GOLDSTON

**Max's brother Sally lived** at the Nafthal farm for many years, later moving for a short period to Felix's farm in Round Hill. He finally made his own home in Dayspring, a village 57 miles (91 km) from Liza and Max's farm.[122] Dayspring was located on the banks of the LaHave River in Lunenburg County, a bedroom community of the neighbouring town of Bridgewater. After the shock of Max's death, the family never saw Sally again.

Sally was the owner of the Bridgewater Lumber Company Ltd. He also founded a stevedoring and forest products export business,

LaHave Traders. Sally loved his adopted hometown and was very popular with its residents. Citizens showed their appreciation for all that he did for the community by honouring him with Bridgewater's 'Citizen of the Year' award in 1976. Bridgewater also named a street after Sally — Nafthal Drive.

Sally never married or had children — it was impossible to find a suitable, single Jewish woman in rural Nova Scotia. He did have a happy life-long relationship and some believe they never married for religious reasons.

Sally was the only member of the Nafthal family to receive compensation from the German government for the loss of his job.

In 1973, Sally Nafthal passed away at the age of seventy-three. At his request, he was buried in the Jewish section of the Strawberry Hill cemetery in Halifax, Nova Scotia.

Max's brother Felix and his wife Lottie sold their farm in Round Hill in 1950. This completed their immigration requirement to farm for seven years. They moved to Bridgetown and purchased the Carleton Inn. Felix and Lottie had two children, Nadja and Axel. In 1965, the couple sold the Carleton Inn and retired to Kentville. Felix and Lottie lived about forty-five minutes from Middleton, but after Max's death the family did not see them again.

Felix was suffering from Alzheimer's when he passed away in 1982 at the age of eighty-two.[123] While Jews do not believe in cremation, Felix was not a religious man and so was cremated.

After narrowly escaping the Holocaust, this marks the end of the Nafthal brothers on Earth. Had they remained in Europe, they almost certainly would have been arrested, sent to a concentration camp, tortured and murdered by the Nazis.

On September 22, 2012, Lottie passed away at the age of one hundred and two. Lottie had spent her retirement years in Kentville where she enjoyed the company of her grandchildren and many friends.[124]

---

Most of the information about Sally reads like an obituary. Sadly, that is exactly where I discovered his life achievements. I always thought Sally was practicing law in Nova Scotia's South Shore. Imagine my surprise to discover he never practiced law in Canada!

I never had the opportunity to know my Uncle Sally. From what I understand, there was a falling out in our family. There are several fragmented stories. Some believe the women in the family fought. Others say the two brothers, Sally and Max, had a terrible disagreement, and that Felix sided with Sally. I like to believe the family would have come together again if Grampy had lived longer. Whatever happened, the sad truth is that the family did break up.

I do have snippets of memories from large Nafthal gatherings on the farm, which included the three brothers and their families. I remember lively, energetic men in suits and ties. I remember ladies wearing simple fashionable dresses, and children running freely without a care in the world. These are the fond but faded memories of a young child; perhaps these images are only a fantasy.

My parents and grandmother never explained the family breakup to me. Everyone was gone. To this day I'm envious of large family gatherings for holiday events and summer vacations.

Much later in life, I did have the opportunity to meet my Aunt Lottie, but she was not interested in getting to know me. My siblings and I also reunited with our cousins, Nadja and Axel. We are good friends now but the warm reunion was bittersweet because we missed our childhoods together.

During the summer of 2019, I had the opportunity to meet with Nadja while I was on a rare visit to Nova Scotia. She seemed surprised I didn't remember much about Uncle Sally. Nadja told me he had been a wonderful uncle to her and Axel. Uncle Sally had always been in their lives and was remembered as a kind and jolly man. I was amazed when I heard this description of my uncle because that is exactly how I remembered him.

Throughout my childhood and adult life, I have felt a great loss. I often wondered what could have been if the family stayed together. Among the missing relatives, I especially missed Uncle Sally, and there were times I wished I'd had the nerve to find him. It wouldn't have been difficult, but I never did. As a young teen, I had grand plans to ride my bike to Dayspring, but my insecurities concerning my memory impairment stopped me. I was young and painfully afraid of rejection, believing Uncle Sally wouldn't want me. After his death, it was too late. Sadly, I'm left to wonder what would have happened if I'd made the move to reunite with my uncle.

My family was here one day, and gone the next day! No one seemed to considered the young children. Without knowing the reasons for the breakup, this will always be impossible for me to understand.

The next time I travel to Nova Scotia, I plan to visit Sally's grave. I'll also drive by his old home in Dayspring and take a walk on Nafthal Drive in Bridgewater and I'll think about the three brothers, Max, Felix and Sally. My next stop will be the tiny community of Round Hill to see where my Uncle Felix purchased a farm and settled in his early years. My last stop will be the Nafthal/Goldston family cemetery; to lay a stone from the beach in my west coast neighbourhood — to say that I was there — and I remember.

Chapter 56

# To Life, To Liza

**As time went by,** Liza's five grandchildren outgrew their rural lives and moved to Halifax, the capital city, where they married and started families of their own. Because the Goldston siblings weren't raised with religion, none of them married into their faith. That was OK with Liza — she wasn't surprised, nor did she care. The only thing that mattered was the healthy arrival of each great-grandchild and the happiness of her growing family.

As Liza grew older, her gut issues persisted. In the mid-1970's she was diagnosed with cancer. The disease often came with a death sentence, and this would be no different. Around this time, Liza, Vera and Joe sold their Middleton homes and moved to Dartmouth, Halifax's sister city, where four of Liza's five grandchildren and their families lived. But the move was difficult for Liza, and she declined quickly.

In less than a year after moving, Liza's cancer had progressed to the point that she was admitted to the Dartmouth General Hospital. It was painful to see her there. She looked so tiny and helpless, not at all who she had been.

Liza drifted in and out of sleep and often seemed confused, or so people thought. The nurses said she was mumbling about concentration camps, smokestacks and gas chambers. Liza was often fearful and restless. Holocaust thoughts haunted her in those last few weeks. The family tried to calm her, assuring her she was safe, but nothing worked. It was Vera who finally discovered the source of her mother's anguish.

From Liza's window, she could see the Nova Scotia Hospital directly across the street. The hospital complex was made up of several brick buildings, including a laundry building with a tall smokestack. In Liza's confusion, or perhaps as a result of her medication, she believed the hospital complex was a concentration camp. In her mind, the laundry building with smoke billowing from its chimney was a Nazi gas chamber. Liza was living in Hell. Vera informed the hospital staff, and they immediately turned her bed away from the window. This calmed her down. On November 6, 1979, Elizabeth (Liza) Isserlin Nafthal passed away peacefully at the age of eighty-one. She was buried in the family plot at the Nictaux Cemetery beside her beloved husband Max.

---

Nanny never talked about the past — the two World Wars, the Russian Revolution, or the Holocaust. She never talked about the friends and family she had lost, nor did she mention the homes, properties, bank accounts and valuables that were gone. My grandmother lived in the present. Still at some point, I realized Nanny's life did not start at my birth. And I always wondered what was behind her silence.

I knew not to ask questions — don't ask me how, I just did. Before I started researching my grandmother's journey, I didn't know anything about WWI or the Russian Revolution. I was naive when it came to connecting my family with the horrific historical events of the pre-WWII years. Resources weren't readily available when I was a child and I would have been too afraid to check out this information anyway. My grandmother believed silence was the best way to deal with her horrific past, and perhaps, for her time, this was right. Nanny could never have dreamt that one day the World Wide Web would provide endless amounts of material about this horrendous period. She wouldn't even think Mom might leave bits and pieces of the horrific family history behind — but she did.

My research and writing have taken me on an emotionally difficult journey into the past. How I wish I could give Nanny one more huge hug. While I can't go back in time to embrace my grandmother, I can share some of the most loving recollections I've gathered as I wrote.

---

## Memories of Nanny

One of the few things my grandmother shared about her past was its link to her persistent gut issues. She often blamed the Russian Revolution for her constant indigestion, a result of near-starvation. I never asked for details, and I should have tired.

Although Nanny was a wonderful cook, in later years she kept her meals beautifully simple. Her favourite meal was the first dish she prepared at Le Cordon Bleu decades before — a humble poached egg on homemade buttered toast. Nanny's other favourites included broiled lamb chops with mint jelly, and poached halibut with cultured butter, topped with a sliced hard-boiled egg. Nanny's Matzo ball soup, with broth so clear one could see to the bottom of the bowl, was everyone's favourite. I loved to eat at Nanny's house.

---

My grandmother was also an avid reader and talented knitter. I never saw her without an open book and a knitting project in progress. I was the only grandchild interested in knitting, and I remember my first big project. Nanny purchased a large bag of beautiful, apple-red yarn so I could knit a sweater. I finally finished the sweater and wore it often, but I'll never forget how many times Nanny ripped out rows of stitches and made me start over again. She told me it was all part of knitting, and I better get used to it. This was so true. To this day, it has never bothered me to rip out rows of stitches.

Heather, my oldest daughter, was fascinated with the tales of how fast Nanny's hands could knit. I'd tell my grandmother I needed a hat for one of my girls to go with a new coat. An hour or so later, she would call and tell me the hat was done. Most times, the hats came with little mittens too! Everything she knit always fitted perfectly. Heather has become a keen knitter too, and I know how proud that would make her great-grandmother.

---

My sister Janet shared this story with me one day. Janet moved to Halifax after graduating from high school and got her first job that summer. Exactly one year later, she was at work on her birthday. Janet was sad because no one knew it was her birthday, and she was homesick. To make matters worse, it was raining outside. As she was working, she looked up to see Mom and Nanny standing at the counter! They had decided to make the two-hour trip to Halifax and take her out for a birthday dinner. It was one of Janet's happiest birthdays ever.[125] That's the way Nanny and Mom did things.

---

My brother Jack had a story about Nanny as well. In 1967, when he was just out of high school, Jack accepted a job as a trainee at the Royal Bank of Canada. He began his training in our hometown of Middleton, where he discovered huge amounts of money were being deposited into our grandmother's bank account. Shortly afterward, the funds would be transferred out of the account and into a business account belonging to her lawyer. This happened time and time again. My brother was very curious and finally couldn't take it any longer. Although he knew he shouldn't ask, he decided to question Nanny about why so much money was flowing in and out of her account.

Nanny was matter-of-fact when Jack asked her about the account. She told him that Grampy had been the executor of the wills for many Jews murdered in the Holocaust. This responsibility then fell onto her shoulders when Grampy passed away. After all these years, she was still working as an executor. When Jack asked how many wills she had worked through, Nanny claimed she didn't know, but the numbers were high. She told Jack that her lawyer was the legal representative for all these claims, and they worked together. Jack told Nanny he couldn't help but notice that she forwarded all the funds to the lawyer, never keeping her executor fee. She agreed. The fees alone added up to a small fortune, and Jack reminded Nanny that she had the right to charge for her work. Nanny smiled and asked why? "These people have already lost so much; it's the least I can do." I could see Jack's pride in our grandmother as he told me this story; a story that truly expresses the love and empathy of Liza Nafthal.[126]

---

In 1978, when my second daughter Sarah was four weeks old, I took her home to meet Nanny. She was the newest addition to the Nafthal/Goldston family. It was winter and I had Sarah wrapped in a blanket in my arms, and my toddler, Heather, at my side. Nanny was by her kitchen sink when I walked in. She rushed to help Heather with her coat. I pushed the blanket away from Sarah's face and Nanny peeked in — fell back and lost her balance. I panicked and reached out, but thankfully my grandmother didn't fall.

"What's happened?" I cried.

Nanny was shaken. "The baby surprised me. She is beautiful!" Then she quickly added, "She looks exactly like you when you were born. It shocked me, that's all. Seeing Sarah's face is like looking back in time."

I knew instantly that it wasn't my face Nanny saw when she looked at Sarah. My baby pictures didn't look at all like my daughter, and she didn't look like her father either. Nanny and I went into the living room so she could sit down. She reached for the baby and cradled her in her arms. "She has inherited a round face like the Russians; so beautiful." I had wondered about the shape of Sarah's face. I waited, but Nanny had nothing else to share.

As I watched my grandmother with the baby, a lump grew in my throat. Nanny seemed so far away; I knew there was much more to her shock than she was telling me. My grandmother was aging, I could see that. I worried, wondering what memories had come back to haunt her as she gently held the newest addition. Was she thinking about a lost one, someone from another lifetime? I believe she was. As Nanny's shock slowly faded, I could see her joy over her beautiful great-granddaughter — and I felt relief. The moment passed, but I never forgot it.

---

I loved my grandmother's hazelnut macaroon cookies. I asked her for the recipe once, but Nan told me she would continue making them for me. When I had more experience as a baker, she would happily give me the recipe. I shouldn't have told Mom this story, because she was furious with Nanny!

The moment Nanny went out, my mother went to her house and wrote down the recipe to give to me. I was mortified — but Mom was very pleased with herself. As I look back now, it was always hilarious to be in cahoots with my mother.

The next time I visited, my grandmother made me a batch of hazelnut macaroons. A week later, the mail carrier dropped off a letter from Nanny. She said I finally had enough experience to bake any of her cookies. I didn't have the heart to tell her I'd already baked her macaroon several times! I tucked the notepaper in the clear envelope of a binder cover I used to store recipes. That way, I can see it often.

---

My grandmother's favourite cousin, Eva, and her immediate family were the only Isserlin relatives to survive the Holocaust. While I was writing this book, I found Eva's daughters — Ilana Zilber-Rosenbury in Israel, and Michal Aizenman in the Los Angles area. Ilana sent me a wonderful memoir Eva wrote when she was ninety years old. Michal wrote me a lovely note and told me she remembers my grandmother clearly. She also remembers her mother's excitement when she would talk about Liza or when she was about to see her. Eva loved doing things with Liza. They cooked together when they visited each other, and Liza taught Eva how to make jam.[127]

Liza's cancer prognosis was not good when Eva made her last visit. Sad as it was for the two cousins, that visit always remained a cherished memory. On the last trip, Liza taught Eva how to knit socks, which Eva knit for her daughter. After forty-three years, Michal still has those socks and sent me a picture. Since Nanny had taught me how to knit, in return, I sent Michal a picture of my latest pair of knitted socks too.[128]

---

I saw my grandmother for the last time the day before she died. It was the first time I felt true helplessness watching someone I love slowly pass away — there was absolutely nothing I could do. Nanny lay peacefully in her bed, but by now she was not waking anymore. She was a shell of who she once had been, and my heart ached for her. I looked out the window for some time, visualizing what my grandmother truly believed she was seeing — a concentration camp. I knew she had never forgotten the horrors of her past.

For decades, Nanny held all her terrible experiences, fears and losses inside. Even after all my research, I still don't know her full story, but I do have a deeper understanding of the period from her birth to her life in Canada. I wish we could visit now. I'd ask questions about her life and hope to finally receive the answers. I'd tell her how much I appreciate all she endured. I'd tell her she is the strongest woman I have ever met. I'd tell her I love and miss her always.

Chapter 57

# Vera, Not Forgotten

> None of my girlfriends survived the Holocaust. All are gone without a trace.
>
> -VERA OLGA (NAFTHAL) GOLDSTON

**Back in 1964 at** the age of forty-five, Joe sold his shares in A.W. Allen & Son Ltd. to retire. He wanted to pursue his lifelong interest in photography, so he attended the New York Institute of Photography for six months. He enrolled in the portrait program with Yousuf Karsh, the world-renowned portrait photographer and instructor. Vera was a stay-at-home mother with five children, but she left the children with their grandmother and housekeeper, Elsie, to join Joe. While Joe was studying photography, Vera registered for an oil colour course. On their return to Middleton, Vera and Joe opened a new business together — Joe Goldston Photography Studio.

Over the next few years, Joe became managing editor of *The Mirror* for Fundy Group Publications, and Vera became the advertising sales manager.

Eventually, Vera and Joe gave up their jobs at *The Mirror*. Vera retired, while Joe accepted a business consultant position with the Federal Business Development Bank, counselling professionals with business start-ups and providing advice to business owners.

Vera and Joe made a wonderful life for themselves after they moved to Dartmouth. They spent springs and summers in Cole Harbour, where they were close to their family and many friends. By now, both Vera and Joe were avid bridge players. Vera made all their square-dancing clothes, enjoyed knitting, and in her later years took up quilting. The couple stayed active in the community with all their interests. Much to the shock of their children, the couple became very interested in the English television soap opera *Coronation Street.*

Once both Vera and Joe were retired, they purchased a motorhome which they drove to Florida and Arizona every winter. They made many friends on their travels, thanks to their love of square dancing and a good game of bridge. They always left on Boxing Day to be in Florida for a New Year's Eve square dancing celebration, and they didn't return until late April or early May.

In the spring of 1987, Vera, now a beautiful, vibrant sixty-three-year-old, caught the flu. At least, that's what the family believed. The flu would last about a week, leave, then come back again in a month. The family tried in vain to convince Vera to see her doctor, but she always refused. As time passed, Vera had the flu more often than not.

Vera's colouring was off — and she also had a hand tremor that was growing worse. It was painful to watch her pick up a few peas with her fork and try to bring them to her mouth. As Vera became weaker, the family continued to pester her to visit the doctor. But Vera thought illness was a sign of weakness and wanted nothing to do with physicians. Eventually, her condition worsened and she had no choice. The moment Vera stepped into the doctor's office, she fell to the floor in a dead faint. She was rushed to Dartmouth General Hospital and quickly admitted.

A few days later, the family received shocking news — Vera had cancer and it had spread to her liver. She was offered chemotherapy, however, this would make her feel extremely sick with no hope of a positive outcome. It was too late. Vera refused all the treatments,only taking medication for comfort and pain relief. Vera finally admitted to her family that she'd known her sickness was much more than the flu. It was not uncommon for Vera to bury her head in the sand, hoping the worst would go away.

Vera was given six weeks to live. The doctors told Vera to get her life in order, and her children and young grandchildren needed to be prepared. She wanted to die in her own home. Joe knew nothing about operating a household or caring for the dying — but no matter. He was determined to take care of his wife and grant her this wish. Joe wanted nothing more than to have Vera close to him until the end.

The only meal Joe knew how to make was fried eggs and chips, English style. The rare occasions Vera was away, Joe would cook this meal for the children and they loved it. Beyond knowing how to prepare fried eggs and chips, Joe couldn't tell you where the salt and pepper shakers were stored in the cupboards.

Joe had never cooked or done laundry or housework, and still, he insisted on taking care of the house and his sick wife! But Vera trusted Joe. In fact, the loving couple had one hundred percent faith in each other. Their adult children agreed and wanted to support their parents. For the first week or so, the couple's daughters prepared meals, and the fridge and freezer began to fill up with Tupperware containers and glass bowls. But Joe was determined. He sat at the kitchen table, the manuals for all the appliances spread out in front of him. When asked what he was doing, his answer was matter-of-fact;

"I'm learning how to use the household appliances!" And he quickly did. After that, the cookbooks came out.

It didn't take long for Joe to reinvent himself as chief cook and bottle washer. He believed cooking and baking were only a matter of following written instructions, and he could do that well. It wasn't long before Joe was wowing his wife and family with gourmet meals, complete with fantastic desserts. His *challah* (Jewish braided bread) was beautiful and far better-tasting than any sold in bakeries. Joe also made the family Christmas trifle with his own special flair. Everything he cooked and baked was delicious and beautifully served, and the family loved it all. Vera could only manage bits of Joe's cooking, but under his care, she held on.

Vera's strength came and went, leaving her a little weaker each time. She had a very strong heart, which kept her going. Her "six weeks" passed, then six months, and Vera was still at home with Joe — and so it continued.

One day towards the end of Vera's life, she was holding an old black and white photograph in her hands. She told her daughter, Peggy, that it was a picture of her friends and classmates from Memel, her old life in Lithuania. As she clutched the photo, she cried. Vera told Peggy she was the only girl in the photo who had survived — all the other girls had been murdered in the Holocaust.[129] They were gone without a trace. All these years, no one knew where Vera had kept the picture. Nor did anyone see it after her death. Joe might have placed the cherished photo with his wife.

On July 31, 1990, Vera Olga (Nafthal) Goldston passed away in her home in Cole Harbour, Nova Scotia. She was far from the place where she'd begun her life, but exactly where she wanted to be. Vera did not give up life easily. She fought for every single breath.

Her death did not come six weeks after her cancer diagnosis, as the doctors had predicted. Instead, she lived for another seventeen months. Following her death, Vera was buried in the family plot of the Nictaux Cemetery, beside her mother and father.

Vera was predeceased by her grandparents, Wolfe and Ella Nafthal, and Eli (Mark) and Olga Isserlin; parents Elizabeth (Liza) and Max M. Nafthal; her aunts, uncles and cousins, murdered in the Holocaust; her son-in-law, Michel; and her young grandson, Jason. Vera left behind the love of her life, her husband Joseph Henry; five children, Janet Pearl, Jack Mark (Linda), Sharon Ellen, Peggy Ann (Wayne), and Max William/ Bill (Muriel); and seven grandchildren, Suzanne, Patricia, Heather, Sarah, Lilith, Lee and Ashley.

It was the end of an era — Max, Liza, and Vera were gone.

---

When my mother received her cancer diagnosis, it was a horrendous shock to the whole family and her many friends. It was even more painful when Mom admitted she'd known all along she was sicker than we believed. She just couldn't face her illness.

Could Mom's early death have been prevented? No one knows. I understand my mother had her ways of dealing with life, and I've accepted that to a degree. Perhaps my mother's knowledge of her sickness should have been another secret Mom took to the grave. But I wonder — maybe Mom's admission was her way of saying that she regretted not going to the doctors sooner, and she was sorry. We will never know.

---

I remember the day my mother died. I remember the call from my older sister Janet telling me the news we had expected, news that would change our lives forever. I listened, hung up the telephone and thought, "Now it's *my* time to forget." And I did forget, for many years. I had learned this strategy from my mother, so the task wasn't as tough as one might expect. But I didn't forget forever — Mom came back to me in her last written pages. I can hear her voice each time I read her words.

When my sister told me about the picture of Moms' girlfriends, I knew the truth. Mom had never forgotten her family and friends murdered in the Holocaust. She never forgot the horrors of her past. I wonder if Mom removed the photograph from its hiding place now and again. Perhaps she'd look at it and remember. I can't begin to imagine Mom's loss for almost everyone she loved at such a young age. Perhaps this was the driving force that inspired her to live life to the fullest. And my mother did live life fully. Maybe Mom lived both for herself and for all her murdered family members and girlfriends. If that is true, they would all be proud — with every breath she took, my mother lived an amazing life.

---

## Memories of Mom

I promised myself I was not going to write about my parents' great love affair, but I know how disappointed they would be if I didn't share at least one story. I believe the following tale is particularly good, as it illustrates who my parents really were and how much they loved each other. This story also reflects the great love between father and daughter.

During the winter of 1948, Dad had a two-week vacation from the family business. My mother put the care of their young daughter, Janet, into the hands of my grandparents. The couple then loaded their old car, took all their cash, and without a destination in mind headed to the United States. As they travelled south, the weather grew warmer. A couple they met along the way suggested they go to Daytona Beach in Florida. Dad was worried about time, but Mom was not concerned. There was no I-95 freeway back then, and Route 1 was a slow drive. When they arrived in Daytona, they immediately fell in love with Florida — a love affair that would last their entire lives.

It took them seven days to arrive at the beach, and while Dad needed to be back in a week, Mom was determined to stay two weeks. So Mom called her father. During the very short call, she told him they were in Florida and staying two weeks. Her father was not pleased, but when he started to speak Mom cut him off by saying that she was hanging up the telephone now. My grandfather had no way to reach his daughter or son-in-law.

Dad was concerned about the reception he would receive on their return, but Mom wasn't one bit worried. Dad thought it might be a different story for him and he could be fired. His worries, however, didn't prevent them from having a wonderful time sunbathing, swimming and enjoying the warm weather. On their way back, Dad had just enough money left for fuel to make it home. There were no credit cards or debit machines in 1948.

My grandfather was furious when the couple finally arrived home, but Mom gave him a huge hug, kissed him on the cheek, and told him what a wonderful time she'd had on the trip. Vati melted. He never said another word, and that's when my father learned the power of a loving relationship between father and daughter.

Mom and Dad spent a month in Florida every winter after that first trip. They left the children home with our grandmother and Elsie and Nelson, the housekeeper and her husband. My parents loved the sunshine and sandy beaches, and the time alone to simply be a beautiful couple in love.

Once Mom and Dad retired, they drove their RV to Florida and Arizona for the winter months — always leaving Boxing Day and returning sometime in early spring. On one occasion, I stopped by their home early on Boxing Day morning to say my goodbyes for the winter. They were supposed to be leaving that morning, but when I arrived there was a note taped on the door. "We couldn't sleep. Left at 2 a.m. See you in the spring! Love Mom and Dad." And that was my parents in a nutshell!

---

Mom wore 'hot pants' when they were in fashion, and she looked fabulous. On special occasions she'd apply apple red lipstick. She'd run a quick comb through her short curly hair and left it at that. Mom never pierced her ears and was furious with me when I pierced mine. My mother was a natural beauty.

She had an enormous passion for Dad — and he loved it. They had no problem showing their affection for one another, which embarrassed me as a teenager. Their love was the standard I used to judge all others — it was part of what kept me single for a very long time.

In the mid-1960s, my parents took up square and round dancing. I remember my father teaching my mother rhythm by tapping the beat on her back over and over again. Once she had rhythm, they became talented dancers. As their love for dancing grew, they rolled up the living room rug and created a private dance studio on the hardwood floor. They'd have two or three squares (four couples in a square) and a square dance caller with a microphone and music. They would dance over our bedroom ceilings late into the night. To this day, I can sleep through anything, anywhere.

Once my husband and grandson couldn't believe I slept on a rough, pitted road in the back seat of an old pickup truck. I have my dancing parents to thank for that!

---

When I was about twelve, Mom taught me how to fry an egg. We used a tiny one-egg frypan. When it started to burn, she yelled, "Grab a plate!" I quickly grabbed the bottom plate and pulled. The pile of plates above came crashing down to the floor — except for the one in my hand. I cried, but Mom hugged me and laughed. I have never forgotten sharing those few precious moments.

---

I remember the day Mom purchased apples from a vendor who came to our door. They were a good price and Mom never turned down a bargain. Later, a town police officer arrived to tell Mom that the apples she'd purchased were stolen. The officer wanted the apples for evidence, but Mom refused to surrender them. She claimed the police would just end up eating her fruit — and that wasn't happening. The officer finally left — without Mom's apples! We teased her terribly about feeding us stolen merchandise.

---

Mom was one of the world's worst drivers — which led to another confrontation with the police. One morning she was working in Bridgetown, a neighbouring community, and was running late. Dinnertime was at noon, however, Mom knew Elsie would have the food on the table. Not wanting to miss a meal with her family, Mom drove a bit more recklessly than usual. The yellow light flashed a warning to stop at the tracks for an oncoming train — but Mom kept going. Two town policemen on the road that day saw my mother. Their siren went off and the cherry on top of the police car flashed. Mom eventually pull over and roll down her window at the officers request. When they asked her to wait while they wrote out a ticket, Mom informed the officers she had no intention of waiting for such foolishness. "I have to get home for dinner with my family," she told them. "If you want to ticket me, you know where I live," and she rolled up the window and drove away!

Just as dinner was being served, Mom rushed into the house, without a word to anyone about the incident. No sooner had we sat down to eat when there was a knock at the side door. Dad went to answer, and from the dining room table, we could hear the cops asking for our mother. My father didn't seem a bit surprised that the police were looking for his wife. Mom got up and joined him at the door. My siblings and I lost all interest in our meal as we listened.

"What's this all about?" my dad asked the police, with Mom standing beside him.

"Vera went through a yellow flashing light at a train crossing in Bridgetown this morning."

"Were you in Bridgetown this morning?" Dad asked Mom.

She shrugged.

"You were!" the cop said to Mom.

Looking for help from Dad, he continued. "And when we stopped your wife and told her we're ticketing her, she refused to wait and just drove away."

Dad looked at his wife. "You did?"

Mom shrugged again.

"We've got a ticket!" the officer said, holding out the paper.

"Do you have proof she was in Bridgetown, or that she didn't stop — maybe a picture?"

"Of course not," said the officer.

"Then how can you give my wife a ticket for something you can't prove?"

The shocked silence at the side door seemed to go on forever! I loved it all!

There was a little more back and forth, and then Dad reminded the two cops that his family's dinner was getting cold on the table. Dad gave them a choice — come in and have dinner, or leave. The officers chose to leave with the ticket still in their hands.

Mom and Dad returned to the table and although there was some giggling and teasing — that ended this great event! There was never a dull moment in our house!

---

Mom was a multi-tasker extraordinaire. In the evening, she would simultaneously knit an intricate pattern, watch television, read a book, and be aware of what all the children were up to. If I hadn't witnessed it over and over myself, I wouldn't have believed it. From time to time, my siblings and I would test Mom, and she always passed with flying colours.

Mom knew exactly what was happening on a television show, the story in her book, and never lost a stitch in her knitting. My grandmother was the same — perhaps she taught my mother, but I can't imagine how! I have never met anyone quite like them.

---

If Mom was waiting for a pot to boil or cookies to bake in the kitchen — she'd play a game of solitaire. Her mind never stopped.

---

I remember the months of sewing, knitting, shopping, wrapping and baking that preceded Christmas. The preparations seemed endless! Mom celebrated the holidays with a vengeance. Years later, the Christmas traditions continued with her grandchildren. Mom made 'goodie boxes' for each grandchild, filled with handmade dresses, knitted sweaters, hats and socks. Mom added toys, games, books and beautiful clothes she found in the States. All the children loved the goodie boxes. My daughter's daycare staff claimed they were the best dressed children there — thanks to my mother!

---

I have a needlepoint Mom made for me. When I moved from the east coast to the west coast of Canada, I removed the frame, and tucked it away in a linen closet for years. During my research, I remembered the art piece and dug it out. When I took Mom's needlework into a shop to be re-framed — all the staff loved it. I hung Mom's needlepoint in my studio, and for the first time in years, I truly looked at it — I am amazed.

---

Mom was an avid reader, and in turn, she allowed her children to read anything, as long as we read. Many of my favourite gifts were books. One spring day in 1966, I took Mom's copy of *Valley of the Dolls* by Jacqueline Susann[130] to school for silent reading in English class. I didn't know that day, but many adults considered the book trash and a bad influence on teenagers. My teacher took one look at my book, grabbed it from my hands, and tossed it out the window.

I was mortified. The moment the school bell rang, I ran outdoors, picked up my book and rushed home. I told my parents what had happened before the school called. They were furious — but not with me. They went to the school and informed my English teacher their children were allowed to read anything they wanted, as long as they read. The next day, Mom wanted me to take the book back to English class, but I refused.

To this day, my siblings and I are all bookworms, and none of us has a 'lazy bone' in our bodies. Mom taught us there was no such thing as boredom, and I thank her for that! It was one of the greatest gifts she gave me. I've carried this lesson through adulthood, and it has enhanced my life beyond imagination.

---

When my siblings and I were sick, Mom made custard. My two sisters live on the east coast just a few minutes away from each other by car —while I live on the west coast. When Peggy was battling cancer and couldn't eat much, my older sister Janet often made our Mom's custard for her. Watching Peggy's long fight against cancer from across the country was difficult. I can't explain the comfort it brought me, knowing Janet made Mom's custard for Peggy.

---

In the spring of 1989, Mom and Dad purchased airline tickets to England for the first time in decades. Dad wanted to visit his childhood home in Blackfriars, London. Then just before leaving, Mom received her cancer diagnosis. Even in the early days, she felt too weak to travel. Mom confided to one of her daughters that she was worried about visiting Europe. She wasn't sure she had legal Canadian citizenship and was afraid she might not be allowed back into Canada. We all thought this was absurd!

In my research, however, I discovered my mother received her citizenship through the Naturalization Act on May 18, 1945. A year later, all immigrants accepted under the Naturalization Act automatically received full Canadian citizenship under the new Citizenship Act. This included my mother and grandparents.

During Mom's illness, perhaps she was confused about the events that had happened so many years before. It's very sad to think that she was doubting her status so close to her death. Mom had always been so proud of Canada and her Canadian citizenship.

---

Nearly four decades after my grandmother sold the farm, the stately house was turned into and inn and restaurant called the Falcourt Inn. When I visited the inn, I was told this story by the owners, the Le Gard family.

The family turned the upstairs kitchen into a guest bedroom with bath. Periodically, a guest would arrive in the dining room for breakfast, and ask if the inn was haunted. When asked why, the guests all claimed the same thing. They would wake in the dark of night to see a form of a woman with short curly black hair and glasses, wearing an apron over her dress and standing in the kitchen.

The Le Gards had found a picture in the attic when they were renovating the inn. They'd show the guest the picture of the woman standing in front of a stove and the guests all agreed — that was the woman they saw the night before. The woman was my mother, Vera. I don't know much about ghosts , but perhaps Mom still visits the old homestead once in awhile.

# Conclusion

*So life goes on, from one generation to the next.*

In 1957, Liza sold Max M. Nafthal Ltd. to Jim Christie, but she didn't sell the name with the business. Max M. Nafthal continued to exist as a company that made trades on the stock market providing Liza with a comfortable living. After Liza's death, the family dissolved the company. The only thing left of the original business in Middleton is the brick office building. The property has been sold numerous times to several different businesses.

The two Nafthal/Goldston homes in Middleton have been sold several times over. They are well cared for properties, showing their owners take pride in their beautiful homes.

Middleton never did buy into large industries. It is still a lovely rural town, which continues to proudly proclaim itself as the "Heart of the Valley."

Liza sold the family farm to a Dutch farming corporation called Bonda Farms — and then in the 1970s — the property was purchased by a German family. Eventually, the land was divided into smaller parcels and sold off. In March 1994, Dianne Hankinson LeGard and her family purchased the Nafthal's former main house and a small parcel of land surrounding the home. Dianne was the daughter of Max's best friend, Tom Hankinson.

The family did a huge renovation, transforming the stately farmhouse into Falcourt Inn. Renovations included adding bathrooms to every guest room, two bathrooms for the restaurant and a huge renovation to Liza's kitchen. Each bedroom door had a copper plaque displaying the room's name. The Nafthal's old bedroom was named "Max's Room." After Vera passed away, the Nafthal/Goldston family had a weekend together at the inn. On that weekend, the family beat the record of drinking the most coffee per capita than any other group!

Owning the old Nafthal home was a dream come true for Dianne. The inn proved to be a successful business, and Dianne was proud to own such a beautiful property. As Dianne approached the age of eighty, however, she decided it was time to sell.

The LeGard family closed the Falcourt Inn on January 1, 2017, and rented the building to Ledgehill EHN Canada, the property's new owners, subject to loan approval. The sale took place on February 15, 2017. Ledgehill EHN Canada now uses the property as an addiction treatment centre for women.

---

When Vera passed away in 1990, Joe remained in their home. It was difficult for anyone to imagine Joe without Vera, but he continued to lead an active life with his family and many friends.

On April 27, 2004, Vera's beloved husband, Joseph Henry Goldston, passed away in the Dartmouth General Hospital surrounded by his family. A few days before he passed, he told his children, "I had a wonderful life; I regret nothing, and I'd do it all over again exactly the same way."

Joe's ashes were buried beside Vera's in the Nictaux Cemetery. Following the interment at the graveyard, a reception was held at the Falcourt Inn.

To this day, the Nafthal/Goldston family plot remains the only Jewish cemetery in rural Nova Scotia — perhaps the only Jewish cemetery in rural Canada. In recent years, the Nictaux Cemetery was in desperate need of more space, and so the family donated the strip of land that bordered the full length of the cemetery. This gift came with two conditions — the church cares for the family site, and that the Nafthal plot remains enclosed by a fence, to satisfy the Jewish laws for burial grounds.

Felix's son, Axel, asked the Nafthal/Goldston family for their blessing to bury his father's ashes in the Nafthal family plot. Felix passed away in 1982 without a place to bury his ashes. The family agreed. Axel knew that his father's ashes were held somewhere in Strawberry Hill cemetery but didn't know where. He asked his mother, Lottie, the whereabouts of Felix's ashes. She had no idea where they were. A quick call to the funeral home and the ashes were located — to the relief of everyone — including the funeral director. The mortician had been waiting patiently for more than twenty years for someone to pick up the ashes. Felix's remains were buried in the Nafthal family plot. In 2012, Lottie was laid to rest beside him.[131]

Max's other brother, Sally, passed away in 1976 and is buried in the Strawberry Hill Cemetery in Halifax. To date, Sally does not have a marker in the Nafthal cemetery plot.

The break between Max and Felix has been reunited and my generation have come to an agreement. Whatever the fight, it had nothing to do with this generation — and after all the old generation is gone. The two families are friends today, however, this too is bitter sweet because there is always the past — and what could have been.

While most of the Nafthal/Goldston family still resides throughout Nova Scotia, the family now extends to British Columbia and California. Everyone looks forward to family reunions, and when they gather, they often bring up the older generation. There is talk, laughter and sometimes tears while family members reminisce about the old days on the Nafthal farm and in the Middleton house.

Liza, Max, Vera and Joe would all be proud of the newest members of the Nafthal/Goldston family — triumphant proof that Adolf Hitler failed in his attempt to eradicate the Jewish race. They are the third generation born after the Holocaust — Joshua (Josh), Tori, Chiara, Teagan, Abigail (Abby), Charles (Charlie), and Winter (Winnie) to date. These young people have brought great joy to the family. One day, they will have the opportunity to talk, read and learn about their ancestors. They will learn where they came from, and what great courage, strength and determination run through their bloodline. Maybe this younger generation will think about their ancestors from time to time, perhaps even research or visit the European countries their family once called home. My wish is that once in a while, they'll talk about Liza and Max, and Vera and Joe.

# Afterword

My mother and grandparents' silence were an attempt to bury the trauma of the past, but it was naïve to think that I wouldn't be affected. I am part of the first generation born in Canada after the Holocaust; I feel its effects, its losses and its pain. The Holocaust robbed me of the mother and grandparents I might have had — just as alcoholism robs a child of the parent they might have had without a drink. The Holocaust robbed me of who I might have been. Most tragically, the Holocaust robbed me of aunts, uncles, cousins and the relationships we might have had, and the lives these individuals might have led.

I believe the pages my mother wrote before her death and her plea not to be forgotten was an invitation to return to the past and recover my family's history. The journey started slowly. I shelved the pages for a year, then took them out and reread them. Bit by bit I organized my mother's material, collected pieces of information, and connected them with historical events. "Just a little research," I thought. "A few short stories. What harm will it do?"

Once I started, I couldn't stop. I emailed museums, libraries and schools in the United States, Europe and Israel. I connected with historians in Europe and Canada and reconnected and met cousins in the United States, Australia and Israel. I chatted with another cousin in Ontario and corresponded with a cousin still living in the Annapolis Valley in Nova Scotia. I sent endless questions to Dianne LeGard, the daughter of my grandfather's best friend. My siblings received countless questions from me, and never once complained. It was a joy to connect with all of these people. With only one exception, I received replies to all my email queries. The recipients didn't always have answers to my questions, but, if possible, they gave me another contact or source to pursue.

I was angry with Mom. I'd blame her for not talking, or leaving enough written information in her pages. The few stories she left behind lack details that I was endlessly hunting down. Most time, however, I silently thanked my mother for mustering up the courage and strength to write the few pages she did. I'm sure it was an extremely difficult task for Mom — but something she obviously wanted to do. I am amazed and proud of Mom and her writings.

Writing this book has taught me to understand and finally accept my family's silence. With so much time having passed, however, now is the time before our family history is lost forever. With my mother's written permission, for the first time in my life, I began to share our family stories. In the beginning, I only shared humorous family stories with my writing community. As a result, I opened up and shared small pieces of my family's horrific journey. It was extremely difficult and painful to share at first. After all, I had never talked of such things before. As time pasted, the reading became easier, but the writing continued to be challenging. My family's story grew as my research deepened. To my surprise, I could see personalities emerging. I was shocked to discovered I had so much pride and love for my ancestors whom I've never knew.

As I continued and discovered so many horrors around my family's lives, I developed symptoms of grief and morning — tears, depression, and sleepless nights. Like my family before me, I grieved in silence. I didn't know how to explain to others that I was morning people who passed decades ago.

One day, I met Rabbi Bentzi Shemtov, Director of Chabad in Nanaimo. He invited me to join a workshop he was facilitating called 'Journey of the Soul: A fresh look at life, death and the rest — in peace.' Rabbi Bentzi taught me a great deal about death and dying and helped me through my grieving process. I learned how to honour my family during my everyday life. Now, I can read pieces of my family's journey out loud to others without crying — most times. I have learned how to remember my ancestors, without the heart-wrenching grief I suffered before.

Today, I have the answers to two questions. First, did I have to live through the Holocaust to suffer its effects? No, I did not have to live through the Holocaust to feel pain for my ancestors or the aftermath of the horrors they experienced. I was born just six years after the Holocaust ended — of course, I feel its effects. And now, for the first time in my life, I give myself full permission to feel that pain and heal.

Second, did I have to know my relatives to mourn them, even after decades? The answer is simple. My ancestors are not just names anymore — they are my family. I do not have to personally know my ancestors to grieve for them. And I have grieved.

My grandparents and parents' generations weren't the last victims of the Holocaust. I once read that the effects of the Holocaust will continue through five generations. I am the first Canadian-born generation, my daughters are the second, and my grandson is from the third generation.

Writing my family's story has been a difficult and emotional experience, and I would do it all over again. I have done my due diligence and stayed true to my mother's last written pages. I have honoured the many shared memories of my grandparents and added historical events so the reader can better understand my family's journey. My mother's writing was not filled with emotion, nor were the few stories she shared over the years. But I am not my mother — I am a passionate and emotional woman, and I could not write without adding passion and emotion to the events I described. I only included facts that I could back up through family, friends and research. *Beach Moose & Amber* is my interpretation of my family's history. Small everyday details are missing, as well as entire months and years of life — and I am sorry for that. The complete story has gone with my ancestors.

This book has been more than an attempt to find my family's Jewish history; it has been a journey of love and passion, and the determination to find that one last, tiny detail. It has been a journey of courage — my courage. It has been a journey of healing — my healing. And finally, it has been a journey of gratitude — my gratitude. Without my mother's last written pages, this book would not exist. Without my grandmother's strength, determination and courage, without my grandfather's money, without my mother's childhood understanding of a deadly situation, and of course, without my father — *I* would not exist.

My wish for *Beach Moose & Amber* is the same as my mother's wish for her last written pages — that one day, in years to come, someone in our family will take an interest in these old stories. Perhaps one day someone will develop a skill for writing and research and incorporate some of my material into another book, with even more information. And in this way, our family will live on.

And now it is time for me to let go and write these last few words.

*Thank you to Nanny and Grampy, Mom and Dad,*
*For the greatest writing adventure of my lifetime — to date.*
*With much love and a promise never to forget,*
*Your loving granddaughter and daughter,*
*Sharon*

THE END

Image 1. Liza in mourning black honoring the death of her parents.

Image 2. Liza's siblings and their family. *Left to right:* Kolia, Mania, Olga, Grisha, Aniela.

Image 3. Liza and Max on the promenade in Holland during the good times.

Image 4. Wolfe Nafthal's home 3 Liepu Street, Memel. The Nafthals owned three homes on the street. The houses were confiscated during the Holocaust — and never returned.

Image 5. Liza and Vera

Image 6. Vera and Max

Image 7. Vera and Max

Image 8. About 1931/32, Vera's grandfather Wolfe Nafthal and Vera shortly before his death.

Image 9. Vera with her favourite Isserlin cousin Eva Kirschner (Cyrinski)

IMAGE 10. Liza and Vera

IMAGE 11. At the beach: Eva Kirschner (Cyrinski) with Vera at about twelve years old.

Image 12. Liza wearing her famous fox stole that she used to smuggle jewelry and valuables across the borders —with her brother, Grisha.

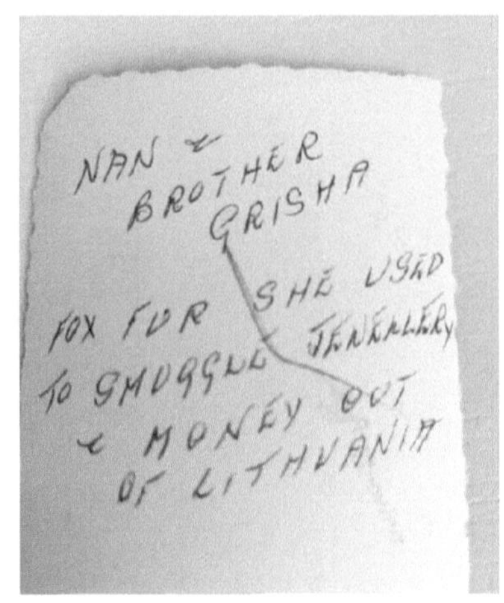


Image 13. Vera wrote on the back of the photograph.

Image 14. Ursula (Ulla) and her sister Hilde before the Holocaust.

Image 15. Albert and his father Nathan during happier times before the Holocaust.

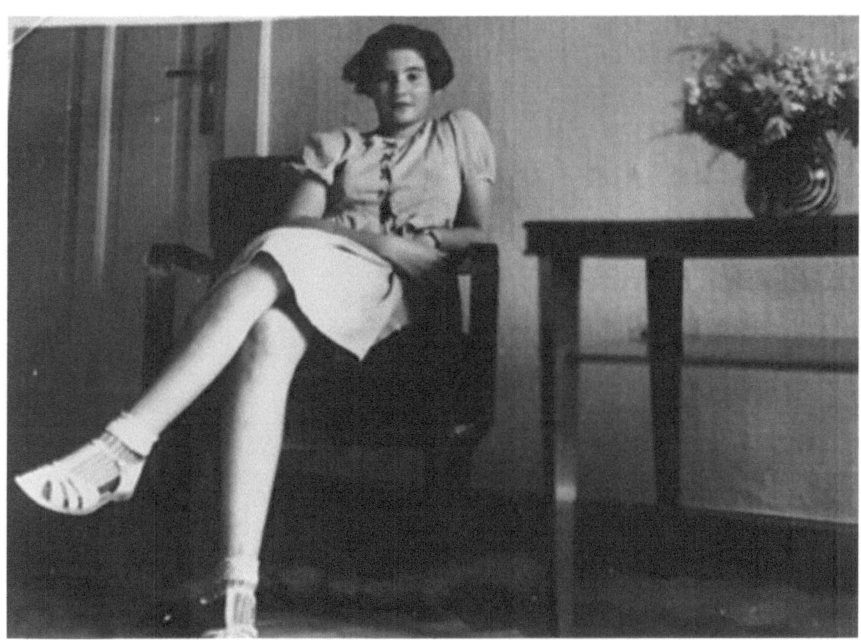

Image 16. Vera in the summer of 1934.

Image 17. Vera in Memel less than two years before she was expelled from school for being a Jew.

Image 18. Liza and Vera sometime during 1939 before leaving Europe.

Image 19. The stately home on the Nafthal farm in Nictaux, Nova Scotia.

Image 20. Liza, Max and Vera on the farm during the late summer of 1939.

Image 21. Vera and Joe in love.

Image 22. Ulla in Germany during post-war years.

IMAGE 23. Max overseeing his crop on the Nafthal farm.

IMAGE 24. Joe and Vera.

IMAGE 25. Max in his Middleton office.

IMAGE 26. The photograph of Vera found in the attic of Falcourt Inn. When guests talked of seeing a silent ghost —they all agreed. This was the picture of the woman they saw.

# Acknowledgments

My deepest gratitude and love for my daughters, Heather Goldston and Sarah Gavin, and grandson, Josh Goldston, for believing in me, and always being there to encourage me on this writing adventure — along with everything else I do in life. When I finally sent my manuscript to my editor, the three of you each said individually, "*I'm proud of you!*" And that meant everything to me. Without you, Heather, Sarah and Josh, there would be no driving force to record my family's journey. I love and appreciate each of you. You are my joy.

With gratitude and love to my husband, Chuck. In the early days, you helped with my research when I got stuck. You made meals when I didn't appear in the kitchen, and you did extra dog duty for our two beautiful pups, Hazel and Gracie. You kept yourself busy with your projects, so I never felt I was leaving you behind while I spent vast amounts of time with my story characters and endless hours writing in my studio. Best of all, you took on the role of my "personal computer geek"; without your support I might still be staring into space, looking above my laptop screen wondering, "How do I fix this now?" Thank you for everything, my love.

To Professor Dr. Ruth Leiserowitz, historian, my greatest appreciation for answering endless questions, both personal and otherwise, about the pre-war years in Memel, Memelland and Lithuania. I would never have found the answers online, in articles or in books. Thank you for helping me understand possible circumstances in an impossible time. Without your contributions, *Beach Moose & Amber* would not be what I was striving to create.

To Professor Peter Gatrell, my warm gratitude for helping me understand the conditions and dangers of travelling in Russia during WWI and the Russian Revolution — an extremely complex era.

To my dear friend Margaret Murphy who was there from the beginning and still is by my side. My warmest love and appreciation for believing in me and my story, for insisting that I create deadlines and for always keeping me on track of what my story is about. A huge thank you for spending countless hours supporting me through the edit check on my final draft as my first reader. Without you, my project would have gone in circles without an end. You are my confidante and my rock.

To Jack M. Goldston, Sharon Styve, Judith Lapadat, Heather Marshall, Gail Madjzoub, Bruce Wagner and Lesley Ripley, I send my warmest gratitude for the roles you played as readers, and a job well done. I thank you for your never-ending support, your strong belief in my writing and your exceptional feedback. You provided me with the confidence I needed to move forward and take the next step. I will forever be grateful for your love for my story and my creativity, and for your belief that my story needs to be shared.

To Rachel Dunstan Muller, my editor, I express my appreciation for your infinite support and strong belief in me and my story. You assured me that *Beach Moose & Amber: Finding My Jewish History* was a worthy read with all the elements I was hoping to create — anxiety, relief, grief, love, understanding and so much more. Your compassion and professionalism were beyond all my expectations. I appreciated your strong emotion and the understanding you displayed towards both my story and my family. Thank you for being a key player on my team and giving me the confidence to move forward into the world of publishing.

To Cindy Folk, my self-publishing consultant who came into my life at the exact moment that I needed her. You took the daunting task of self-publishing and creating an online presence fun and exciting for me. I will never forget your kindness when you called me on a Friday evening because I thought I had lost my Facebook page. I wish you boundless success in your writing and self-publishing consulting ventures and I am so grateful to have you on my team and in my life.

To Sarah Lahay, my book designer from Reedsy, with great appreciation for taking the time to know my manuscript to provide me with the perfect design choices that best suited the atmosphere, reading experience and the people I wrote about. Thank you for answering all my questions, concerns and providing me with your professional guidance. I love my designs!

A tremendous thank you to my writing community, *The Five W's (Whacky, Wonderful, Wise, Wild Writers)* of Nanaimo BC; the *Canadian Foundation of University Women (CFUW) Writing Group* (Nanaimo, BC, branch); *The Salish Sea Writers* of Vancouver Island, BC; and *The Oceanside Writers,* also of Vancouver Island. In the beginning, I suffered through dreadful anxiety as I held back my tears and forced myself to read personal family stories that I had never previously shared. With a lump in my throat, this was an extremely difficult task. I didn't believe anyone would be interested. I believed the opposite; that you would be horrified that I would even bring up the topics of war, the Holocaust and my family's heritage. But you asked for more. You gave me your kind understanding from the moment I first broke my family's silence. You gave me the confidence to give my family's story a voice. You gave me the courage to keep moving on. Thank you for your valued critiques, unconditional support and your true interest in watching my story slowly unfold.

Many warm thanks and deepest appreciation for responding to all my endless questions whether you had an answer or not, to Janet Imbeault, Peggy Brinton, Bill Goldston, Axel Nafthal, Sharon Dobkin, Tamy Rosenbaum, Yoram Rosenbaum, Michelle Aizenman, Ilana Zilber-Rosenberg, John S. Jaffer, Dianne Hankinson Le Gard, Sue Beasley and John MacFarlane. I hope you enjoy *Beach Moose & Amber,* for you have contributed to my story beyond what you realize.

For always asking about my story every time we talked, many thanks and appreciation to Noel Lewis-Watts, Joyce Alexewich, Anthea Marcus, Ann Ronald, Sue Beasly and Jeorge McGladrey. A special thank you to Sandy Cole and Laurie Hutchinson (assistant designer) who not only asked often but listened and critiqued my stories from the very beginning. Every one of you gave me the drive to keep going.

I am grateful to the many people who responded to my endless emails from libraries, museums and private businesses in Canada, the United States, Europe and Israel. It was truly a wonderful experience to receive your notes with answers and references. Thank you for your time and interest in my family's journey.

A huge thank you to all my family, friends, acquaintances, and people I've met along the way for taking an interest in my story. There are too many to mention, but you know who you are.

It takes one person with an idea to begin a story, however, it takes a team to complete the journey. Every one of you is a valued member of my team — *Team Sharon* in *Beach Moose & Amber: Finding My Jewish History*. Enjoy!

# Endnotes

1. Wikimedia Commons, Europe 1929 – 1938 Political Map.svg., *Wikimedia Commons* https://commons.wikimedia.org/wiki/File:EUROPE_1929 1938_POLITICAL_MAP.svg
2. Wikimedia Commons, Rzeczpospolite Central Lithuania.png., *Wikimedia Commons,* https://commons.wikimedia.org/wiki/File:Rzeczpospolita_Central_Lithuania.png
3. World Atlas, recent Map of Nova Scotia, https://www.worldatlas.com/maps/canada/nova-scotia.
4. *Liza*, pronunciation Leesa
5. Wikipedia, Isserles Moses, *Wikipedia*, https://en.wikipedia.org/wiki/Moses_Isserles.
6. *Yahrzeit* is Yiddish and means 'anniversary of a parent or other close relative.'
7. The *Star of David* is a symbol of Jewish identity composed of two overlaid equilateral triangles that form a six-pointed star.
8. *His Master's Voice* (HMV) was the name of a major British record label created in 1901 by The Gramophone Co. Ltd. On February 5, 2019, the Canadian retailer Sunrise Records announced its buy-out of this company.
9. *The Thomas Hedley Soap & Candle Company* was later bought out by Procter & Gamble.
10. *Konigsberg Castle* in the port city of Konigsberg was an important waypoint into Prussian territory.
11. *Kosher* is a term used to describe food that complies with the strict dietary standards of traditional Jewish laws.
12. *Bolshevik* comes from a Russian word meaning "one of the majority." Bolsheviks were members of the majority faction of the Russian

Social Democratic Party, which was renamed the Communist Party after seizing power in the October Revolution of 1917.

13. Wikipedia, Nicholas Il of Russia, *Wikipedia* https://en.wikipedia.org/wiki/Nicholas_II_of_Russia.
14. *Gypsies*: a derogatory term today, but common in those days for Romanians.
15. Gatrell, Peter, Professor, University of Manchester, England, personal communication.
16. Wikipedia, Russian Revolution, *Wikipedia* https://en.wikipedia.org/WW /Russian_Revolution
17. Ibid.
18. Ibid.
19. Gatrell, Peter, Professor, University of Manchester, England, personal communications
20. Wikipedia, Russian Revolution, *Wikipedia* https://en.wikipedia.org/WW /Russian_Revolution
21. Ibid.
22. Gatrell, Peter, Professor, University of Manchester, England, personal communication.
23. *Memel* is known as Klaipeda today; it is the third-largest city in the country.
24. *Memelland* is now known as the Memel region. It is part of Lithuania, however, they have their own borders — a complicated situation.
25. Schwartzort was renamed and is now Juodkrante.
26. *Servia* is now called Serbia.
27. *Zoppot*, Poland, was later renamed Sopot.
28. Goren Cherie, *A Time to Keep: A Memoir of Growing up in Memel.* (Unpublished memoirs).
29. Ibid.

30. Ibid.
31. Ibid.
32. Ibid.
33. Ibid.
34. Kirschner, Eva *Let's Rather Laugh*. (Not published memoirs).
35. Ibid.
36. 'Coloured' refers to members of the ethnic Black community.
37. United States Holocaust Memorial Museum; "Timelines of Events", United States Holocaust Memorial Museum, https://www.ushmm.org/learn/timeline-of-events/1933-1938/death-of-german-president-von-hindenburg.
38. Ibid.
39. Leiserowitz Ruth, Prof. Dr.
40. Ibid.
41. Ibid.
42. Ibid.
43. Ibid
44. *Yom Kippur* and *Rosh Hashanah* are Jewish High Holidays.
45. Leiserowitz Ruth, Prof. Dr.
46. Ibid.
47. Ibid.
48. *Kike* is an insulting and contemptuous word for a Jewish person.
49. Brinton Peggy, my sister, personal conversation.
50. Brinton Peggy, personal conversation.
51. Wikipedia, The Evangeline Conference, *Wikipedia,* https://en.wikipedia.org/wiki/%C3%89vian_Conference.
52. Ibid.
53. Britannica, The Munich Agreement, *Britannica*, https://www.britannica.com/event/Munich-Agreement.

54. Leiserowitz Ruth, Prof. Dr.
55. Goldston, Jack M., my brother, personal conversation.
56. Leiserowitz Ruth, Prof. Dr.
57. Ibid.
58. Ibid
59. History, Paul von Hindenburg, Autor; History com. Editors, *History,* https://www.history.com/topics/world-war-i/paul-von-hindenburg.
60. Leiserowitz Ruth, Prof. Dr.
61. Ibid.
62. Wikipedia, Kristallnacht, *Wikipedia* https://en.wikipedia.org/wiki/Kristallnacht.
63. Ibid.
64. Ibid.
65. Leiserowitz Ruth, Prof. Dr.
66. Ibid
67. Ibid.
68. Ibid.
69. Ibid.
70. Ibid.
71. Ibid.
72. Ibid.
73. Ibid.
74. Ibid.
75. Ibid.
76. Imbeault Janet, my sister, personal conversation.
77. The Canadian Encyclopedia, The St. Louis, *The Canadian Encyclopedia*, https://www.thecanadianencyclopedia.ca/en/article/ms-st-louis.
78. CBC News, Wheel of Conscience, *CBC News,* https://www.cbc.ca/player/play/1755148178.

79. The Canadian Council for Refugees, None Is Too Many, *The Canadian Council for Refugees* https://www.edu.gov.mb.ca/k12/cur/socstud/foundation_gr6/blms/6-2-4f.pdf
80. CBC News, Justin Trudeau's apology for the MS ST. Louis, *CBC News* https://www.cbc.ca/player/play/1364593219585.
81. Claims Conference, New Survey by the Azieli Foundation Conference Finds Critical Gaps In Holocaust Knowledge Azrieli Foundation, *Claims Conference*, Canada, 2019. https://www.claimscon.org/study-canada/.
82. Claims Conference, New Survey by the Azieli Foundation Conference Finds Critical Gaps In Holocaust Knowledge Azrieli Foundation, *Claims Conference*, quote: Azieli Naomi.
83. An Allied Staging Area, White James F.E, PhD, *Halifax, Nova Scotia in WWII: An Allied Staging Area.* https://hmhps.ca/pdf/Halifax-Nova-Scotia-in-World-War-II-An-Allied-Staging-Area.pdf
84. Ibid
85. *Shul* means 'school' in Yiddish. In this case, it's a religious service, held on the Jewish Sabbath.
86. The *Jewish Sabbath* means a day of celebration as well as one of prayer. Sabbath falls on the seventh day of the week, Saturday.
87. CBC News, Hitler Book maps "Final Solution in Canada,' Library and Archives Canada curator says, *CBC News*, https://www.cbc.ca/news/canada/ottawa/hitler-book-library-and-archives-canada-1.4989961.
88. Built-in 1903, MacDonald School was the first consolidated school in Canada.
89. Halifax Nova Scotia in World War II An Allied Staging Area, White James F.E, PhD, *Halifax, Nova Scotia in WWII: An Allied Staging Area.*https://hmhps.ca/pdf/Halifax-Nova-Scotia-in-World-War-II-An-Allied-Staging-Area.pdf.

90. Leiserowitz Ruth Prof. Dr.
91. Nova Scotia Archives, An Eastern Coast Port': Halifax in Wartime, 1939-1945, *Nova Scotia Archives,* 'The Censor and the City: H.B. Jefferson Captures Wartime Halifax, https://archives.novascotia.ca/eastcoastport/results/?Search=ch3.
92. Imbeault Janet, personal conversation.
93. Hankinson Le Gard Dianne, family friend, personal conversation.
94. Ibid.
95. Ibid.
96. Wikipedia, CFB Greenwood, https://en.wikipedia.org/wiki/CFB_Greenwood.
97. Hankinson Le Gard Dianne, personal conversation
98. *Shabbat* means 'He rested,' signifying the day that God rested from creating the world. The seventh day of the week, Saturday; is a day of peace and holiness.
99. The Lend-Lease Act stated that the US government could lend or lease, rather than sell, war supplies to any nation deemed vital to the defense of the US. The planes were part of this act.
100. Nafthal Freedman Ursula, *Ulla's writings*, unpublished.
101. Ibid.
102. Ibid.
103. Ibid.
104. Ibid.
105. Ibid.
106. Ursula's information: Norm Freedman and Ulla's diary, unpublished.
107. Wikipedia, Vilna Ghetto, *Wikipedia,* https://en.wikipedia.org/wiki/Vilna_Ghetto.
108. Wikipedia, Kovno Ghetto, *Wikipedia* https://en.wikipedia.org/wiki/Kovno_Ghetto.

109. Wikipedia, Dachau Concentration Camp, *Wikipedia*, https://en.wikipedia.org/wiki/Dachau_concentration_camp.
110. Wikipedia, Stutthof Concentration Camp, *Wikipedia* https://en.wikipedia.org/wiki/Stutthof_concentration_camp.
111. Wikipedia, Stutthof Concentration Camp, *Wikipedia*, https://en.wikipedia.org/wiki/Riga_Ghetto.
112. Huguenots: a branch of Protestants that had been persecuted at the end of the Middle Ages by the Catholic French majority.
113. Two Alekhine Interviews (1941) Edward Winter, https://www.chesshistory.com/winter/extra/alekhine5.html.
114. Alexander Cukierman, Professor Emeritus of Economics, Tel-Aviv University and Interdisciplinary Center Herzelyia, Israel. The short version of Julia and Joseph.
115. The World Holocaust Remembrance Centre, About the Yad Vashem Archives. https://www.yadvashem.org/visiting.html?gclid=Cj0KCQjwxIOXBhCrARIsAL1QFCZ-4Bx4jgo3Wd3QCsB3Ls6cNaqyAlzr4DMcqQsozvN8X98j0c10y7oaAlbqEALw_wcB.
116. A Jewish cemetery has physical boundaries that set it apart from its surroundings, making it holy for Jews. A Jewish cemetery is considered consecrated ground where Jewish burial practices and customs are observed.
117. The *Chevra Kadisha* is a group of Jewish men and/or women who perform the final rites and prepare deceased Jews for burial according to Jewish tradition.
118. Imbeault Janet, personal conversation.
119. Goldston Jack M., personal conversation.
120. Sturmann Tamy, my grandfather's niece, personal conversation.
121. Hankinson LeGard Dianne, personal conversation
122. Nafthal Axel, Felix's son, personal conversation

123. Ibid.
124. Ibid.
125. Imbeault Janet, personal conversation.
126. Goldston Jack M., personal conversation.
127. Aizenman Michal, my grandmother's great-niece, personal conversation.
128. Ibid.
129. Brinton Peggy, personal conversation.
130. *The Valley of the Dolls* was the bestselling novel of 1966. To date, it has sold more than 31 million copies, making it one of the bestselling works in publishing history.
131. Goldston Jack M., personal conversation.

# About the Author

Sharon Easton is among the first generation of Jews born after the Holocaust. Her birthplace was rural Nova Scotia, Canada, where her Jewish grandparents and mother immigrated after they fled their home in Lithuania — arriving in Canada six weeks before World War II was declared.

Her family didn't talk about those horrendous years in Europe. Decades after her grandparents and parents passed away, she found her voice and shares her family's experiences. Sharon, her daughters and grandson are three generations of living testimony that the insane determination to eliminate all Jews worldwide during the Holocaust — The Final Solution — failed.

Always a storyteller, when Sharon was too young to know how to write she would take her father's yellow-lined paper and worn pencils to scribble indecipherable sentences while she made up stories in her head.

Adventure was calling Sharon when she moved from Canada's east coast to British Columbia's west coast. One of her goals was to create a writing community around her. Sharon is the co-founder of The Five W's Writing Circle, co-founder of The Salish Sea Writers and a member of the Federation of University Women's Writers. She is also a member of the Federation of BC Writers.

Sharon's first creative non-fiction book titled *Beach Moose & Amber: Finding My Jewish History* is the greatest writing adventure of her life — at least for now.

If Sharon is not in her studio writing, you can find her hiking with friends and dogs, cycling back roads, wandering the beaches or paddling the bays of the Pacific Ocean. She also loves RVing in North America and flying to far-away destinations. Sharon lives by the sea on beautiful Vancouver Island with her husband and two wonderful Labradoodles.

sharoneaston.com
sharoneastonauthor
sharoneastonauthor

To inquire about booking Sharon Easton for a speaking engagement please contact her directly at sharoneastonauthor@gmail.com.

www.ingramcontent.com/pod-product-compliance
Ingram Content Group UK Ltd.
Pitfield, Milton Keynes, MK11 3LW, UK
UKHW041858190726
13854UKWH00002B/961